Table of Contents

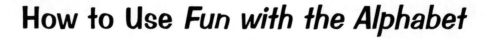

How to Use *Fun with the Alphabet*

Follow these steps to teach letter names and sounds using *Fun with the Alphabet:*

1. Decide on the letter you wish to teach. The alphabet need not be taught in order. Take advantage of events to stimulate interest in a specific letter. If, for example, your class won a pizza party for being the best citizens in the cafeteria, what a great time to teach "P."

2. Refer to the teaching ideas on pages 4 and 5. Here you will find suggestions for how to introduce any letter or sound.

3. Decide which of the activities for that letter you will use. The wide variety of activity choices is described below.

Types of Pages for Each Letter

Large Letter and Picture Cards

• Reproduce a specific letter page, color it, and laminate to use to introduce the letter.
• Reproduce all of the letters and display them in alphabetical order throughout the year.

Learn It!

This page lists the resources for each letter.

Read It!

The bibliography page contains a list of alphabet books plus stories that contain characters or items beginning with the letter/sound being practiced. (With a few books, you will need to select only those pages which are appropriate for your class.)

Eat It!

You will find suggestions for tasty treats beginning with each letter of the alphabet. Some of these can be made by students, others need to be prepared by an adult in advance.

Draw It!

Each letter has a guided drawing lesson to help students create simple pictures from basic shapes. Have students follow along as you demonstrate each step required to make the picture. Extend these drawing experiences by having students add a background that makes the picture tell a story. An oral language experience extends the lesson even farther.

Write It!

These reproducible forms ask students to trace and write capital and lower case letters. Each page contains an additional "fun" type of activity - coloring, connect the dots, drawing. If you are using a different form of writing, cover the letters with an example of the form you are using before reproducing the page.

Make It!

Students make a variety of projects from paper. Step-by-step directions are provided as well as reproducible patterns where needed. The projects require a variety of cutting skills (fringing, rounding corners, spirals). Have students practice these skills using scratch paper, newspaper, or paper scraps.

Other Reproducible Pages

• Cut–and–paste pages for identifying pictures that begin with a specific sound.
• Little story books to read together and take home.
  Each book is printed on one page which, when folded, becomes a simple four page story. You will need to teach students how to fold the books (see illustration).

fold - 1

fold - 2

Additional Resources

Mini-Alphabet Book

Reproduce pages 266 - 272 for each child doing the activity. This mini-book contains an animal for each letter of the alphabet. Students can color the animals and practice reading the letter and naming the animal on each page. Complete directions for making the book are found on page 266.

Games

Pages 273 and 274 contain directions for several games children can play to practice naming letters and giving letter sounds.

Centers

Beginning on page 275 you will find directions for setting up five different centers for practicing letters and sounds. Patterns are included where necessary.

Letter and Picture Cards

Pages 279 - 304 contain reproducible cards. These cards can be used in a variety of ways:
• to introduce letters and/or sounds
• for matching capital and lower case letters
• for matching pictures and letters/sounds
• for sorting into sets by sound

Basic Directions for Introducing a Letter or Sound

Here are some activities you can use with any letter you are introducing. Select those which are the most appropriate for your students.

Letter Names

Use Alphabet Books

Share one or more alphabet books with your students. After reading the books, return to the page dedicated to the specific letter you are studying. Ask students to name the letter. Discuss what picture is used to represent it.

Use Students' Names

Show a card containing the capital and/or lower case letter you wish to introduce. Say the name. Ask students to repeat it after you. Say "Who has a name that begins with this letter?" Have those children stand. Write their names on the chalkboard and underline the first letter. Then look around the classroom for other words beginning with the same letter. Select a child to go to the word and point to the letter being practiced. If no one in class has a name beginning with the letter, provide a stuffed animal with a name tag beginning with the letter being studied. (Xavier Bear will come in handy when you are studying "X"!)

Make Letter Charts

Make a chart representing the letter you are studying. Post a large sheet of paper. Provide a supply of magazines and newspapers, scissors, and paste. Have students find examples of the letter you are studying. They are to cut out the letter and paste it to the chart. This helps students to become aware of the many different ways a letter might look in print.

Write the Letter

After students have learned the name of a letter, begin practicing the strokes for writing it. Have students trace the letter in the air, write it in damp sand, make it out of clay, write on the chalkboard, and practice on paper. It helps some students to say the strokes of a letter as they make it. Utilize as many learning modalities as possible to help students with this skill. Reproduce the *Write It!* form provided for the letter. Give directions for the extra "fun" task at the top of the writing pages.

Letter Sounds

Read a Book

Select a book from the bibliography (or a favorite of your own) containing characters, objects, or other words beginning with the sound you wish to emphasize. Read the story to your students. Then reread it, page by page, and have students listen for those words. Write them on a chart. Then point to the first letter in each word, asking students to give its name and/or sound.

Brainstorm

Show a letter card and say the sound the letter makes. Students repeat the sound. Ask "What starts with this sound?" Write the words named on a chart. Point to each word and read it aloud. Have students repeat it. Ask a child to underline the letter you are studying. (Put a picture after each word if possible to help students when they "read the room.")

Sort "Stuff"

Use real objects (or plastic models) for students to sort by sound. Develop a collection of small items you can access as you practice a sound. Students can listen for one sound as they name the items (putting things with the sound in one set and objects that do not have the sound in another set) or sort all of the items by their beginning sounds.

Use Picture Cards

Reproduce the picture cards (pages 279 - 304). Laminate and cut them apart. Use these as you introduce each individual sound and to review a group of previously introduced sounds.

Make an Alphabet Book

Have students make their own page each time you study a new letter or sound. Have them write the capital and lower case letter and draw an appropriate illustration. Display these during the time you are studying the letter. Provide a file folder for each child to store the pages . When all letters have been introduced, put each child's pages in order and add a cover. They can take these personal alphabet books home. (This is a time-consuming task. Call on helpful parents and older students to help organize the pages.)

6

Pages four and five provide teaching ideas for introducing and practicing each letter. Use these in conjunction with the specific resources for "A" listed below.

Have students sort objects. Put things starting with the sound "a" makes in the pockets of an apron.

Note: Determine whether you will introduce both the short and long sounds of the vowel at the same time.

Alphabet Books

A is for Antarctica by Jonathan Chester; Tricycle Press, 1995.

ANTics! An Alphabetical Anthology by Cathi Hepworth; Putnam, 1992.

Applebet An ABC by Clyde Watson; Farrar, Straus, & Giroux, 1982.

Books About Apples

Apples by Rhoda Nottridge (Foods We Eat Series); Lerner Group, 1991.

Apples and Pumpkins by Ann Rockwell; Simon & Schuster, 1989.

Albert's Field Trip by Leslie Tryon; Simon & Schuster, 1993.

Apples, How They Grow by Bruce McMillan; Houghton Mifflin, 1979.

Apple Picking Time by Michele B. Slawson; Crown Books for Young Readers, 1994.

Apple Tree, Apple Tree by Mary Blocksma; Children's Press, 1983.

Books About Ants

Ant by Steven Savage; Thompson, 1995.

Ant Cities by Arthur Dorros; Crowell, 1987.

Anthoy Ant's Creepy Crawley Party by Lorna Philpot & Graham Philpot; Random House, 1995.

Cuidades de hormigas (*Ant Cities* in Spanish) translated by Daniel Santacruz; HarperCollins, 1995.

If You Were An Ant by S. J. Calder; Silver Press, 1989.

Two Bad Ants by Chris Van Allsburg; Houghton Mifflin, 1988.

- 2 pounds (450 gms) tart cooking apples
- 1/2-2/3 (100 - 134 gms) cup sugar (depends on tartness of apples)
- 1/2 cup (118 ml) water

1. Wash, core, and pare the apples; cut into quarters.

2. Put water into a saucepan. Bring to a boil, add apples, and bring back to a boil.

3. Reduce heat, simmer 20-25 minutes. Stir occasionally. Add water if needed.

4. Stir in sugar until well combined. Serve warm or cold.

Enjoy applesauce with animal crackers and milk.

 Draw It!   # The Ant

Direct students to fold a blank piece of paper into four sections. Draw on the chalkboard and use oral instructions to guide students to draw the following:

1. Make a red ant.
2. Make an angry red ant.
3. Make a red ant on a green leaf.
4. Make a red ant going uphill.

Oral Language Experience:

Students dictate a sentence or short story about one of the pictures to an adult.

Aa

name

black

red

green

Trace and write.

a a a a a a

A A A A

apple   ant

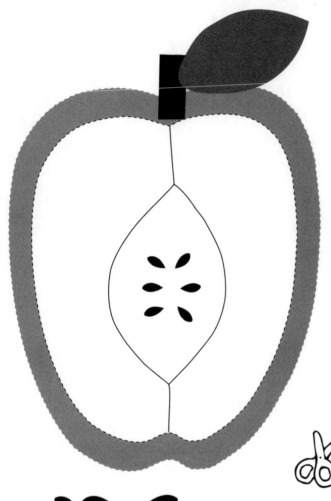

Materials:

- reproducible pattern (page 12) on red, green, or yellow construction paper
- reproducible pattern (page 13) on white construction paper
- scissors
- paste
- 1" x 2 1/2" (2.5 x 6.25 cm) brown construction paper for a stem
- 2" x 3" (5 x 7.5 cm) green construction paper for a leaf

Optional:

- real apple seeds

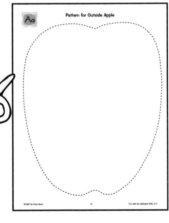

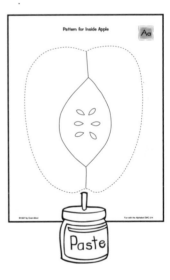

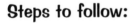

Steps to follow:

1. Cut out the patterns.

2. Paste the inside of the apple on the outside of the apple leaving a colored border.

3. Cut a leaf from the green rectangle.

4. Paste the leaf to the brown stem.

5. Paste the stem on the back of the apple.

6. Color the seeds brown or glue on real apple seeds.

Pattern for Outside of Apple

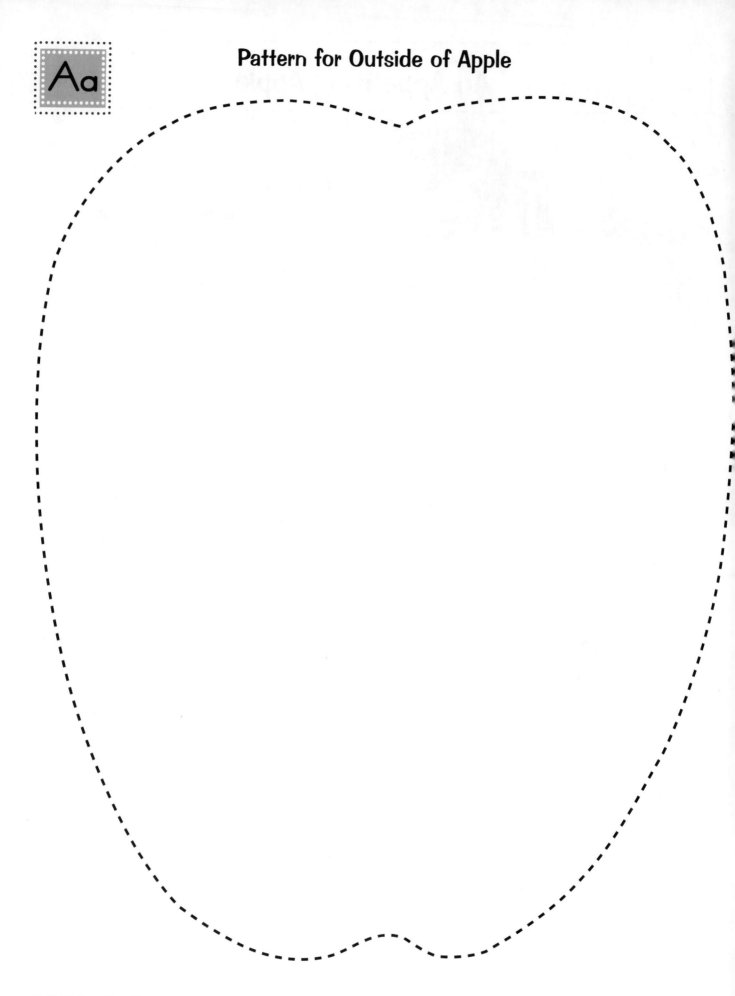

12

Pattern for Inside of Apple

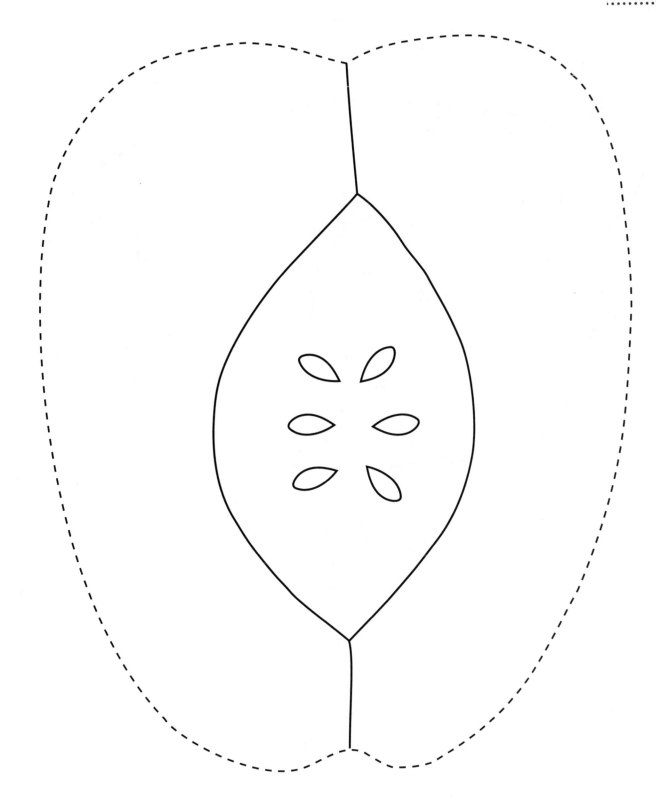

Fun with the Alphabet EMC 774

Fill the Basket

name

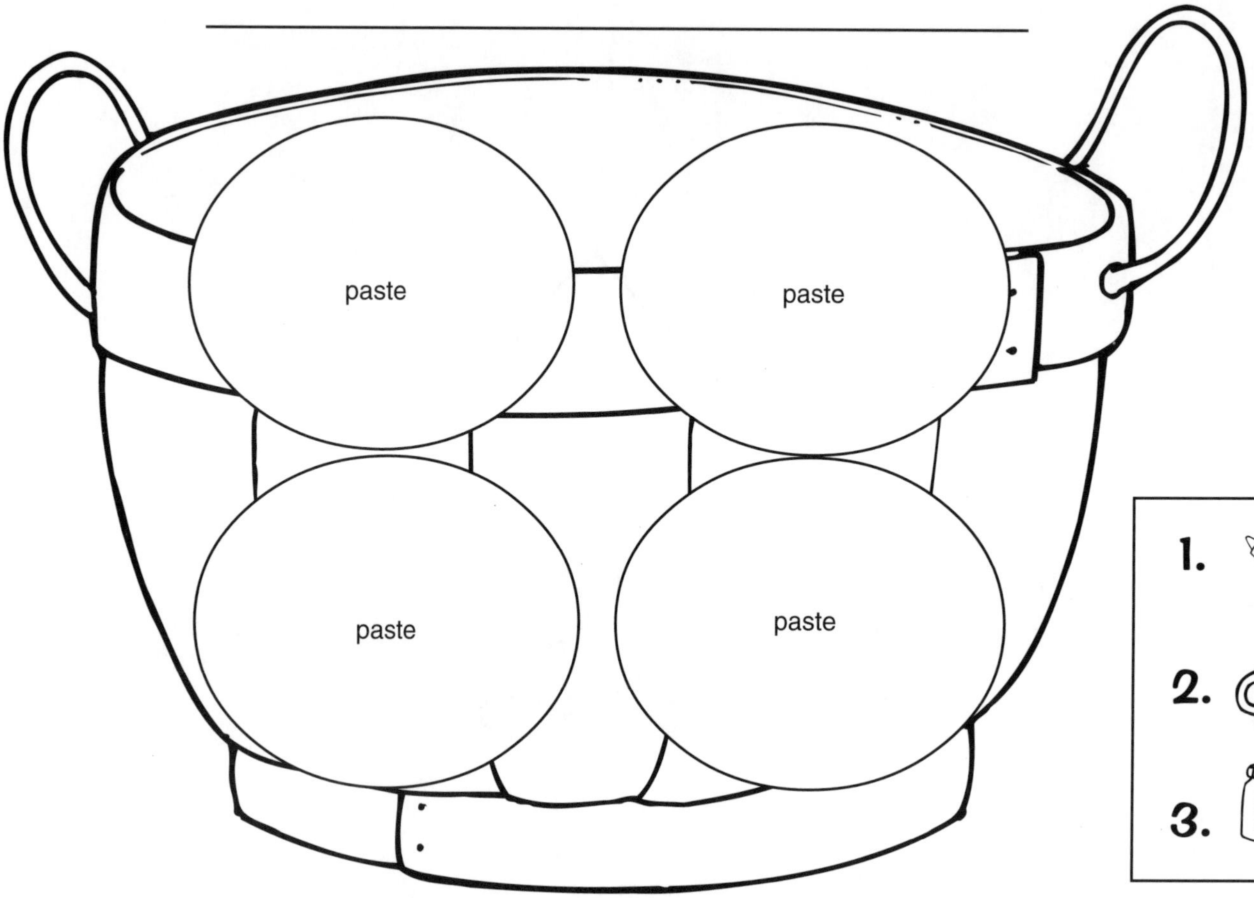

paste paste

paste paste

1.  ✏️

2.  ✂️

3.  Paste

14

Fun with the Alphabet EMC 774

An ant took my apple.

The Ant

①

Aa

②

fold 1

I had it for a snack.

fold 2

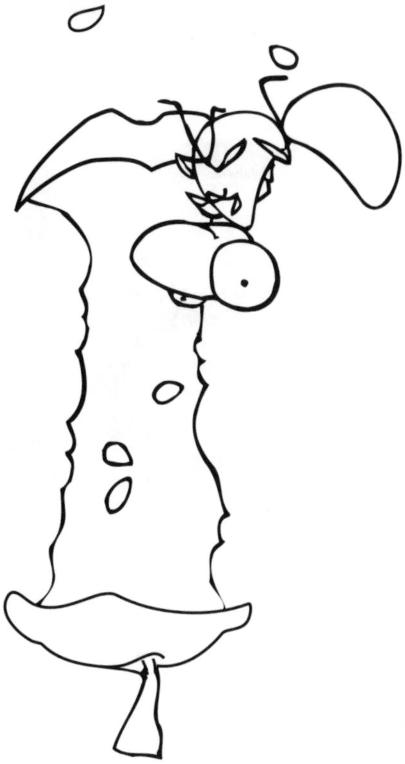

I want my apple back!

④

③

An ant took my apple.

16

Fun with the Alphabet EMC 774

Pages four and five provide teaching ideas for introducing and practicing each letter. Use these in conjunction with the specific resources for "B" listed below.

Have students sort objects. Put things starting with the sound "b" makes in the basket.

Alphabet Books:

Ben's ABC Day by Terry Berger & Alice Kendell; Lothrop, Lee & Shepard, 1982.

The Birthday ABC by Eric Metaxes; Simon & Schuster, 1995.

teddy bears a b c by Susanna Gretz; Macmillan, 1986.

Books About Bears:

Bears by Raymond Briggs; Random Books for Young Readers, 1994.

Bears in Pairs by Niki Yektai; Bradbury Press, 1987.

Bear Play by Miela Ford; Greenwillow Books, 1995.

Bedtime for Bear by Sandol Stoddard; Houghton Mifflin, 1985.

Big Bad Bruce by Bill Peet; Houghton Mifflin, 1977.

Brown Bear, Brown Bear, What Do You See? by Bill Martin, Jr.; Holt, Rinehart, & Winston, 1983.

Edward in Deep Water by Rosemary Wells; Dial Books for Young Readers, 1995.

"I Don't Care!" said the Bear by Colin West; Candlewick Press, 1996.

It's the Bear! by Jez Alborough; Candlewick Press, 1995.

Peace At Last by Jill Murphy; Dial Press, 1980.

We're Going On A Bear Hunt by Michael Rosen; McElderry Books, 1989.

Books About Balloons:

The Blue Balloon by Mick Inkpen; Little, Brown, 1990.

Brown Rabbit's Shape Book by Alan Baker; Kingfisher Books, 1994.

Harvey Potter's Balloon Farm by Jerdine Nolen Harold; Lothrop, Lee & Shepard, 1993.

The Red Balloon by Albert Lamorisse; Doubleday, 1957.

Too Many Balloons by Catherine Mattias; Children's Press, 1982.

 **Eat It!**   # Butter and Bread

Make butter

- 1 pint (474 ml) whipping cream
- 1 large jar and lid
- Yellow food coloring
- Salt to taste

1. Pass the jar of whipping cream around the room, letting each child shake it 20 times. Add salt and coloring when it is the consistency of whipped cream. Continue until a lump of butter forms.

2. Rinse the butter in cold water until the water is clear.

Have a bread–tasting party with your homemade butter.
     toast
     bagel
     rye crisp
     cornbread
     tortilla
     scone

 Draw It!   # The Balloon

Direct students to fold a blank piece of paper into four sections. Draw on the chalkboard and use oral instructions to guide students to draw the following:

1. Make a big, bouncy, red balloon.

2. Make a beautiful, little blue balloon.

3. Make two balloons. One is purple and one is orange.

4. Make a big yellow balloon with red polka dots.

Oral Language Experience:

Students dictate a sentence or short story about one of the pictures to an adult.

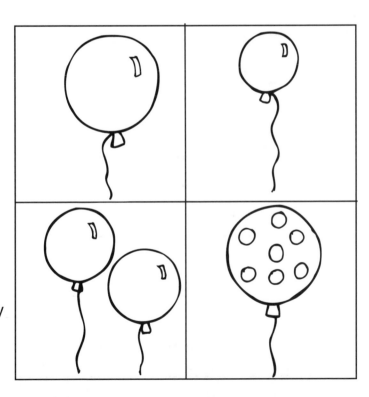

Bb

name

name

Write It!

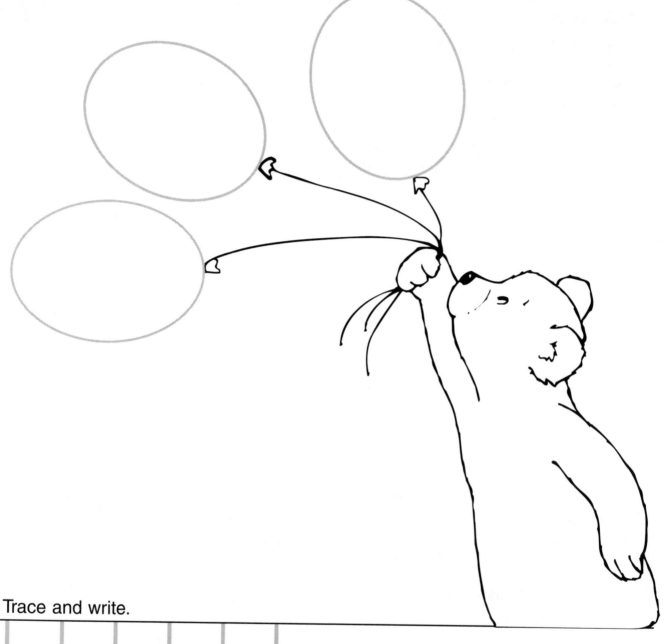

Trace and write.

b b b b b b

B B B B B

bear balloon

Make charming polar bears and brown bears from this easy pattern.

Materials:

- reproducible patterns (pages 22 and 23)
- construction paper
- scissors
- paste

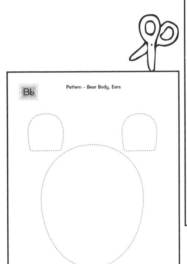

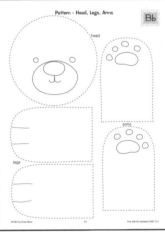

Steps to follow:

1. Cut out all the body parts.

2. Paste the bear together:
   Paste the head on the body.
   Paste the ears on top of the head.
   Paste the arms and legs on the bear with the rounded edges forming paws.

Hint:
Create a hanging decoration for your room by stapling the bears paw to paw to make bear chains.

       Fun with the Alphabet EMC 774

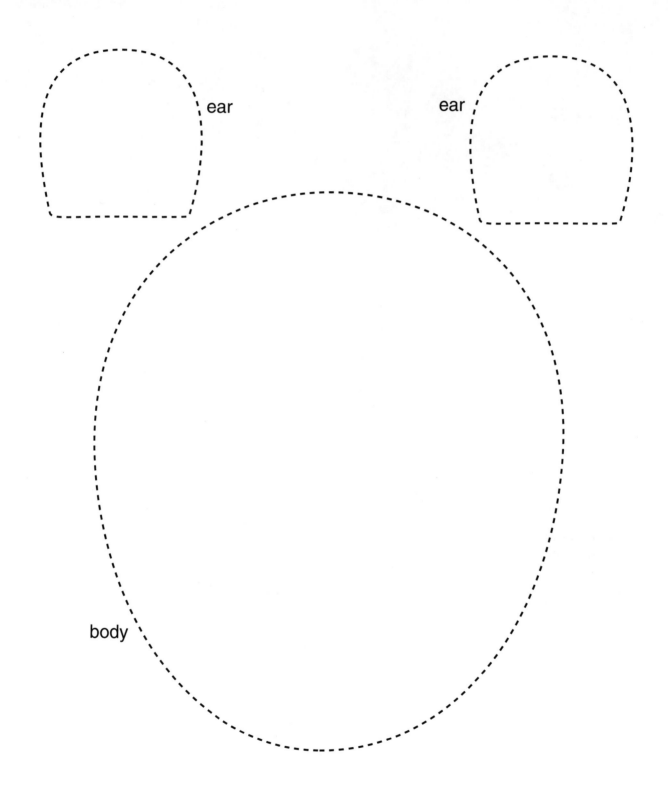

ear

ear

body

Fun with the Alphabet EMC 774

Pattern - Head, Legs, Arms

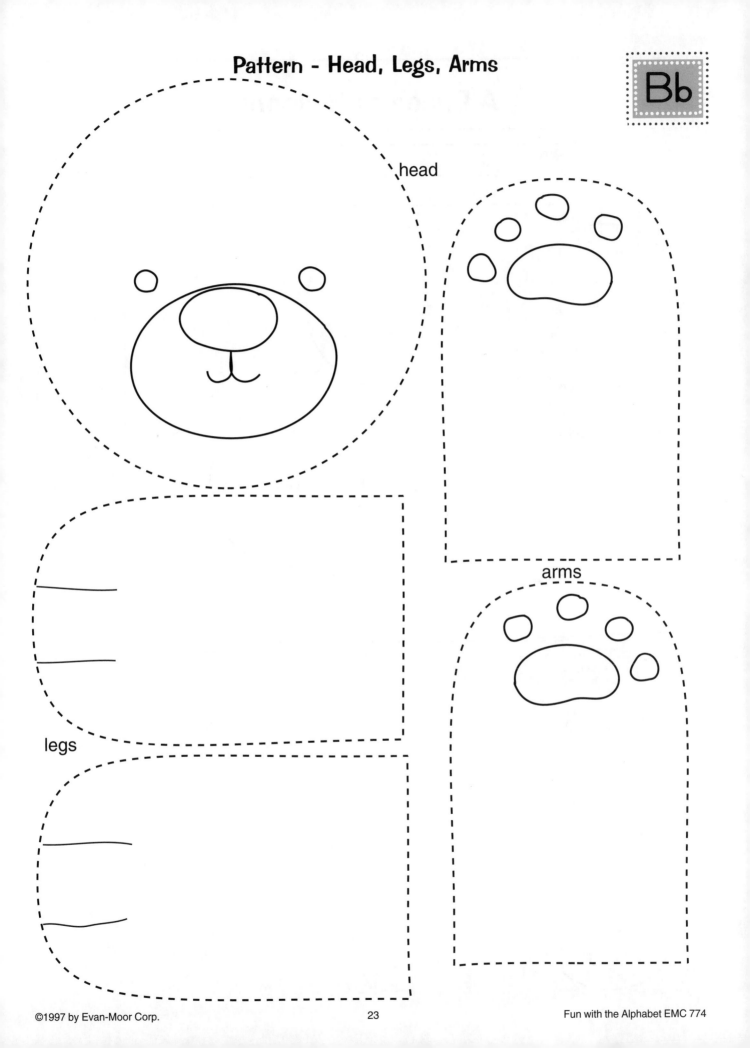

head

arms

legs

Fun with the Alphabet EMC 774

A Bunch of Balloons

name

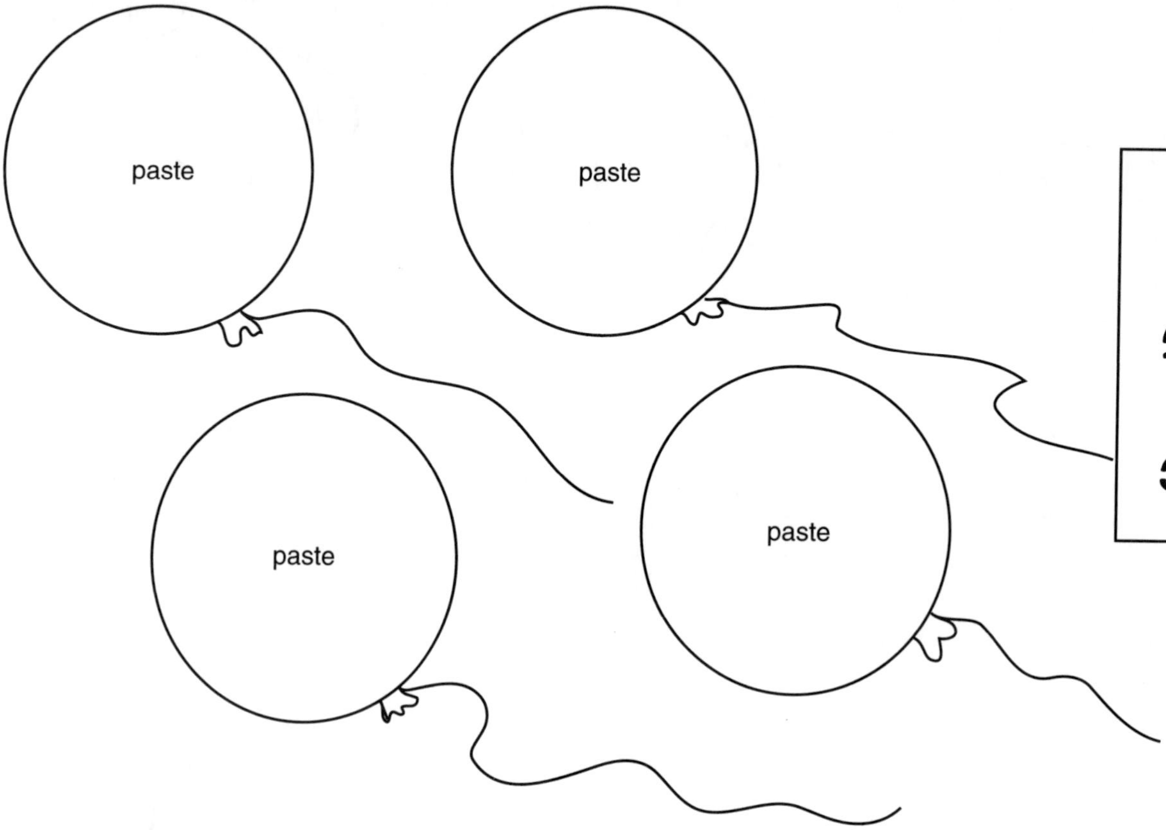

paste

paste

paste

paste

1.
2.
3. Paste

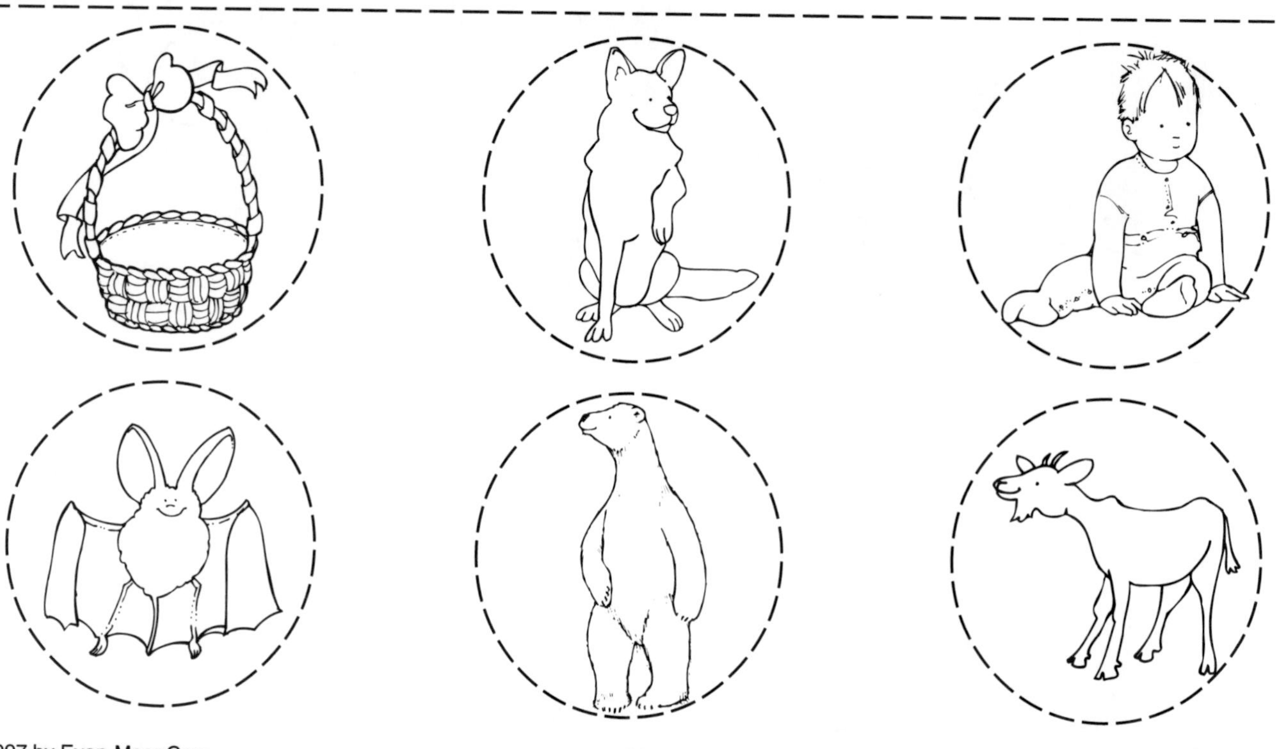

(1)

Baby Bear, Baby Bear,
go upstairs.

Baby Bear

Bb

(4)

Baby Bear, Baby Bear,
say good night.

(2)

Baby Bear, Baby Bear,
say your prayers.

(3)

Baby Bear, Baby Bear,
turn out the light.

Teaching the Letter

Pages four and five provide teaching ideas for introducing and practicing each letter. Use these in conjunction with the specific resources for "C" listed below.

Have students sort objects. Look for real things starting with the sound "c" makes.

Alphabet Books:

Cat's ABC by Josie Firmur; Western Publishing, 1994.

C is For City by Nikki Grimes; Lothrop, Lee & Shephard, 1995.

Jeremy Kaloo by Tim Mahurin; Dutton Children's Press, 1995.

Books About Cats:

Aunt Nina and Her Nephews and Nieces by Franz Brandenberg; Greenwillow Books, 1983.

Cats Big and Little by Beatrice Fontanel; Young Discoverers Library, 1991.

A Cat's Body by Joanna Cole; Morrow, 1982.

Chato's Kitchen by Gary Soto; Putnam, 1995.

Come On Up! (A Giant First Start Reader) by Joy Kim; Troll Associates, 1981.

Cookie's Week by Cindy Ward; Putnam, 1988.

Counting on Calico by Phyllis Limbacher Tildes; Charlesbridge, 1995.

Grandma's Cat by Helen Ketteman; Houghton Mifflin, 1996.

Henry and Mudge and the Happy Cat by Cynthia Rylant; Bradbury Press, 1990.

Nicky Upstairs and Down by Harriet Ziefert; Viking Kestrel, 1987.

The Wee Little Woman by Byron Barton; HarperColllins, 1995.

Books About Cookies:

The Biggest Cookie in the World by Linda Hayward; Random House, 1995.

The Doorbell Rang by Pat Hutchins; Greenwillow Books, 1986.

Larry and the Cookie (A Rookie Reader) by Becky Bring McDaniel; Children's Press, 1993.

 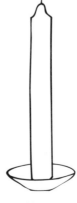 

Cool Custard

- Prepare packaged custard mix or your favorite custard recipe.

- Try some warm cocoa with your cool custard.

 Draw It!

Cookies

Direct students to fold a blank piece of paper into four sections. Draw on the chalkboard and use oral instructions to guide students to draw the following:

1. Make a chocolate chip cookie.

2. Make a peanut butter cookie.

3. Make a smiling cookie.

4. Make a cookie with a bite out of it.

Oral Language Experience:

Students dictate a sentence or short story about one of the pictures to an adult.

Fun with the Alphabet EMC 774

Cc

name

_ _ _ _ _ _ _ _ _ _ _ _ _ _ _ _ _ _ _ _

Trace and write.

C C C C C

C C C C

cookie   cat

Cute Cat

This cute cat gives a lot of practice in cutting circles and spirals.

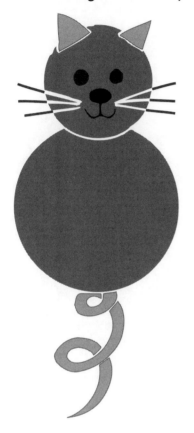

Materials:

- reproducible patterns (pages 32 and 33)
- construction paper
- for whiskers - long pine needles, yarn cut in 3" (7.5 cm) lengths, long toothpicks, or broomstraws
- scissors,
- paste and glue
- crayons
- glue

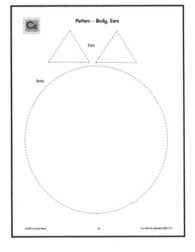

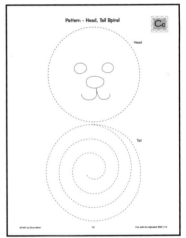

Steps to follow:

1. Cut out the pattern pieces.

2. Paste the head onto the body. Add the ears.

3. Cut the tail circle into a spiral. Paste one end of the spiral on the bottom of the back side of the body.

4. Glue on the whiskers. (Paste is not strong enough to hold the whiskers in place.)

Hint:

To display these cats, punch holes in the top of each head. Tie on strings and hang the cats around the room.

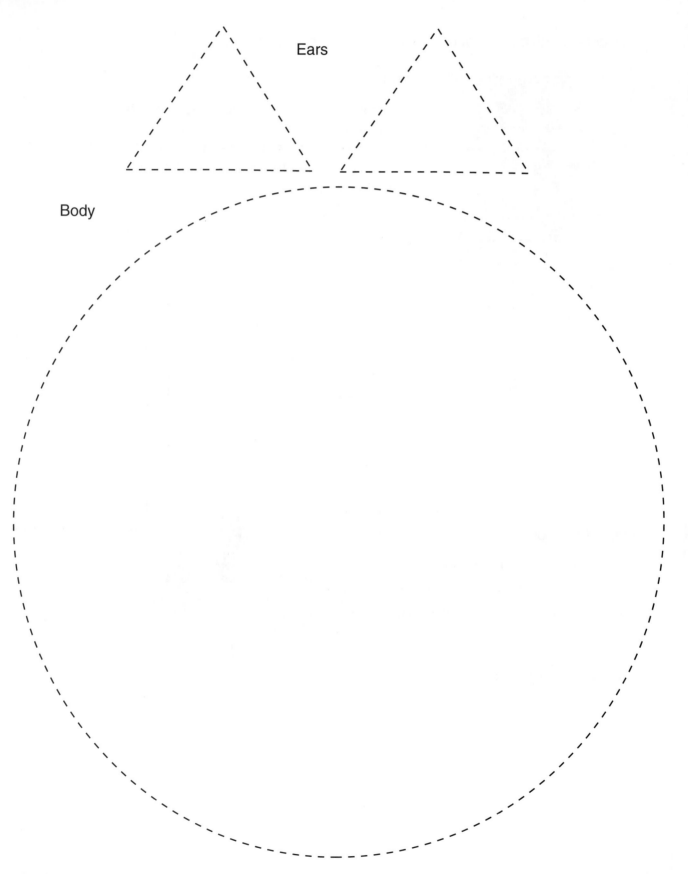

Ears

Body

Fun with the Alphabet EMC 774

Pattern - Head, Tail Spiral

Head

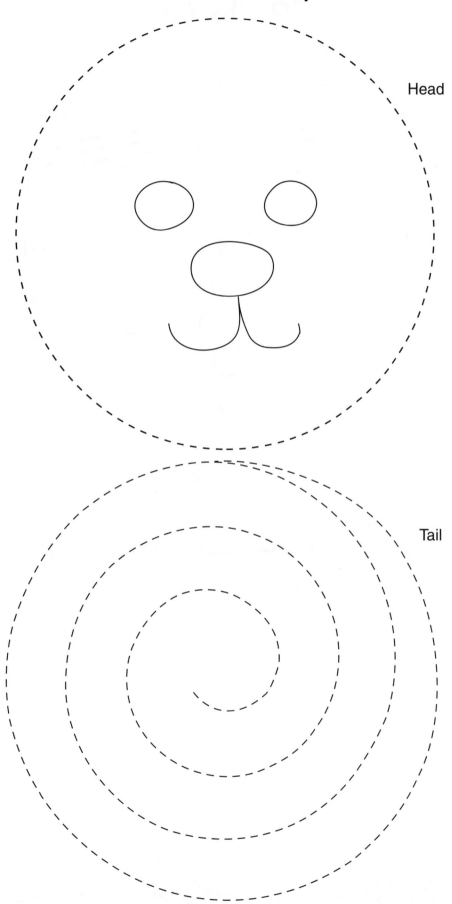

Tail

Fill the Can

name

1.

2.

3.

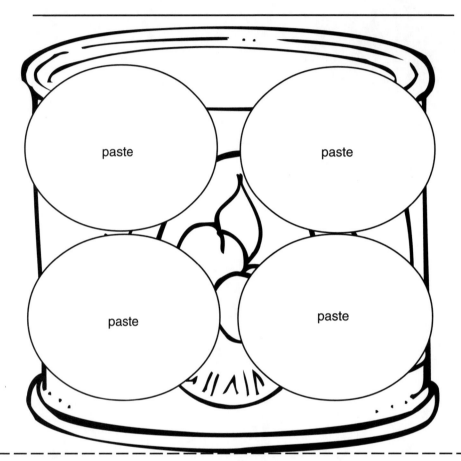

paste

paste

paste

paste

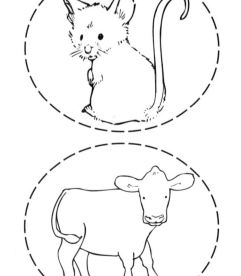

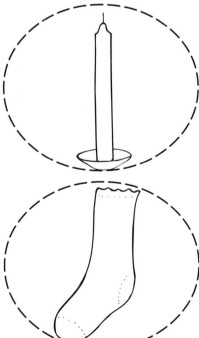

Cookie is my pet cat.

It's time for a nap.

fold 2

4

1

My Cat

Cc

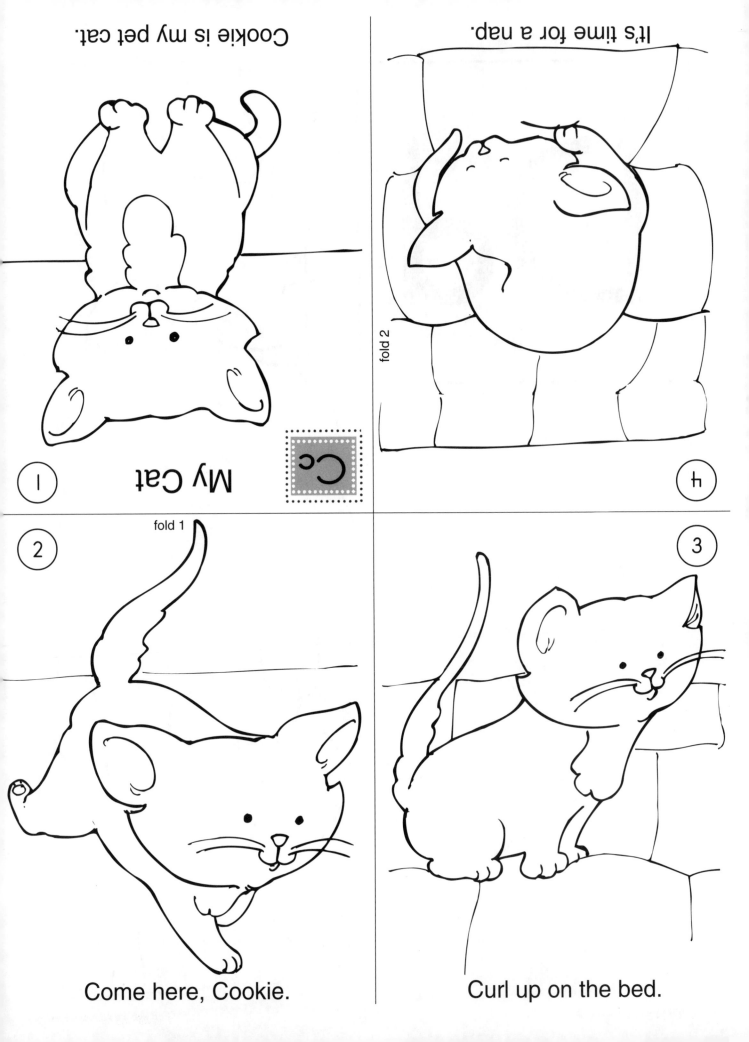

fold 1

2

3

Come here, Cookie.

Curl up on the bed.

Fun with the Alphabet EMC 774

 **Learn It!**

Teaching the Letter

Pages four and five provide teaching ideas for introducing and practicing each letter. Use these in conjunction with the specific resources for "D" listed below.

Have students sort objects. Put things starting with the sound "d" makes in a dishpan.

Alphabet Books:

Albert's Alphabet by Leslie Tryon; Atheneum, 1991.

David McPhail's Animals A to Z; Scholastic, 1988.

The Dinosaur Alphabet Book by Jerry Pallotta; Charlesbridge, 1991.

Books About Dogs:

Angus and the Cat by Marjorie Flack; Doubleday, 1989

Clifford's Kitten by Norman Bridwell; Scholastic, 1984.

Dogs by Elsa Possell; Childrens Press, 1981.

The Dog Who Cried Wolf by Nancy Coffelt; Gulliver, 1995.

Finders Keepers by William Lipkind & Nicolas Mordvinoff; Harcourt Brace, 1951.

Murphy and Kate by Ellen Howard; Simon & Schuster, 1995.

My First Puppy by Rosmarie Hausherr; Four Winds Press, 1986.

Spot hace un pastel (*Spot Bakes a Cake* in Spanish) translated by Teresa Mlawer; Putnam, 1995.

Books About Doughnuts:

One Whole Doughnut...One Doughnut Hole (Rookie Reader Series) by Valjean McLenighan; Children's Press, 1982.

Recipe for dragon's milk:

1. Put milk in a pan.
2. Warm the milk.

Or...get a dragon to breathe on it!

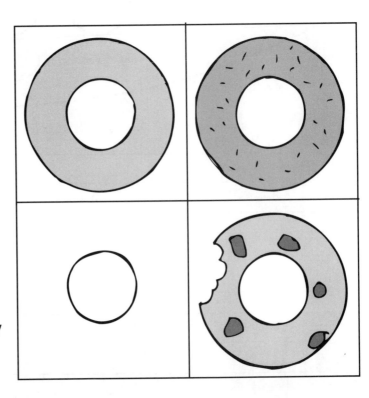

 Draw It! **Doughnuts**

Direct students to fold a blank piece of paper into four sections. Draw on the chalkboard and use oral instructions to guide students to draw the following:

1. Make a delicious doughnut.
2. Make a dunking doughnut with red sprinkles.
3. Make a doughnut hole.
4. Make a blueberry doughnut with a bite out of it.

Oral Language Experience:

Students dictate a sentence or short story about one of the pictures to an adult.

Dd

name

 **Write It!**

Make 2 🦴 in the dog 🥣 .

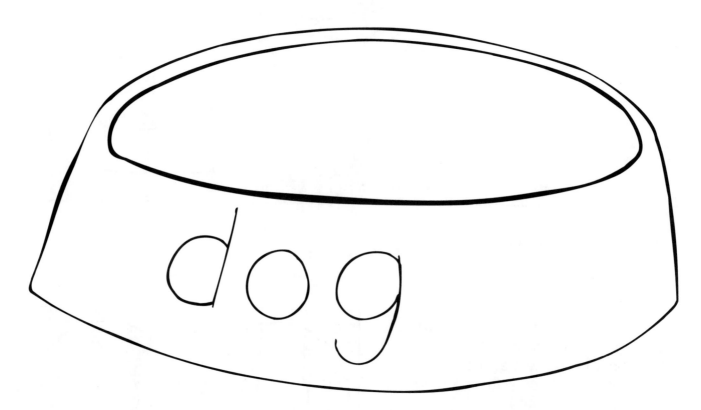

Trace and write.

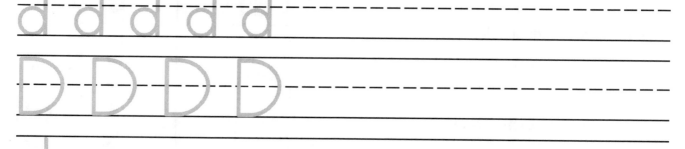

Practice the sound of the letter "d" as you make this delightful dog. Your children will learn to cut fringe at the same time.

Materials:

- reproducible /patterns (pages 42 and 43)
- light brown construction paper
- black construction paper
  1 - 1 1/2" (4 cm) square for nose
- scissors
- paste

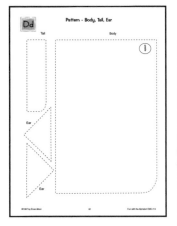

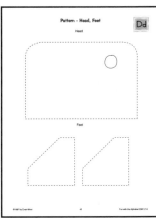

Steps to follow:

1. Cut out the pattern pieces.

2. Fringe the bottom edge of the body, head, feet, and tail by making small cuts (about 1" [2.5 cm] long) with the tip of the scissors.

3. Paste the head on the square, unfringed corner of the body.

4. Paste on the ear, feet, and tail.

5. Round the 1 1/2" (4 cm) black square into a circle for the nose.

6. Paste the nose in place. Note that the nose sticks out beyond the edge of the head.

Pattern - Body, Tail, Ears

Tail

Body

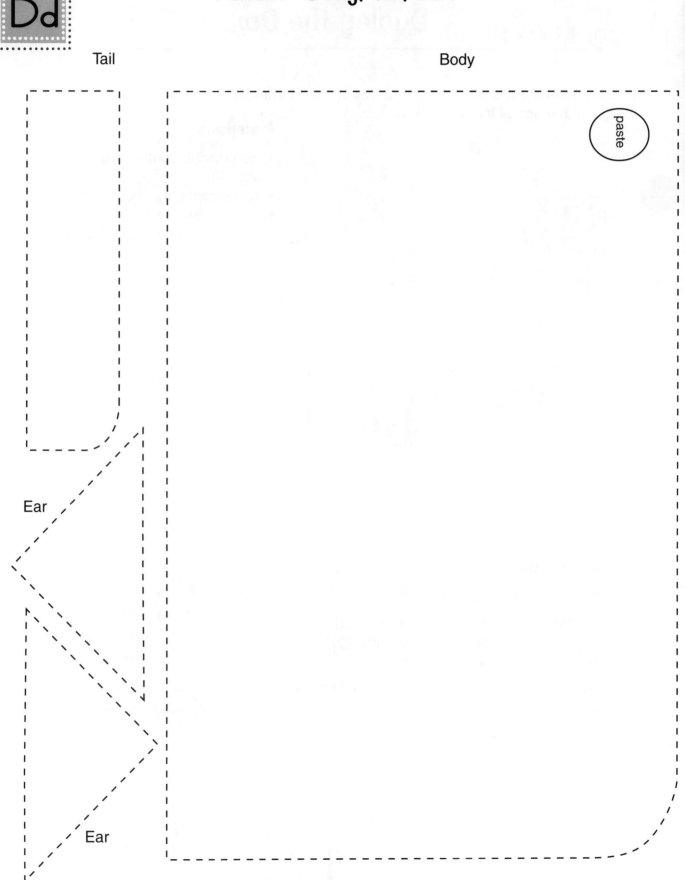

paste

Ear

Ear

Pattern - Head, Feet

Dd

Head

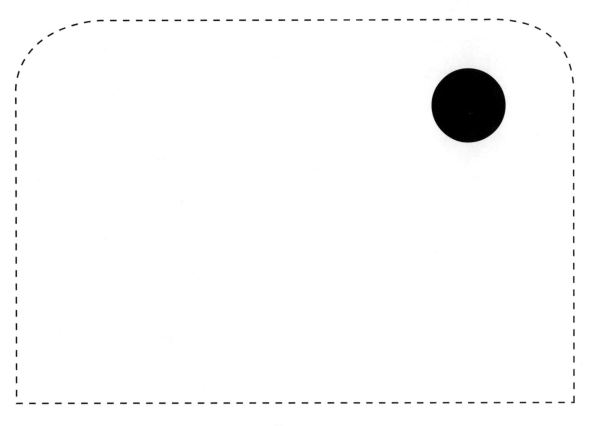

Feet

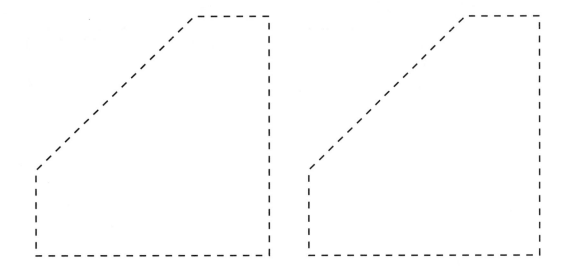

Doggy's Dish

1.
2.
3. Paste

name

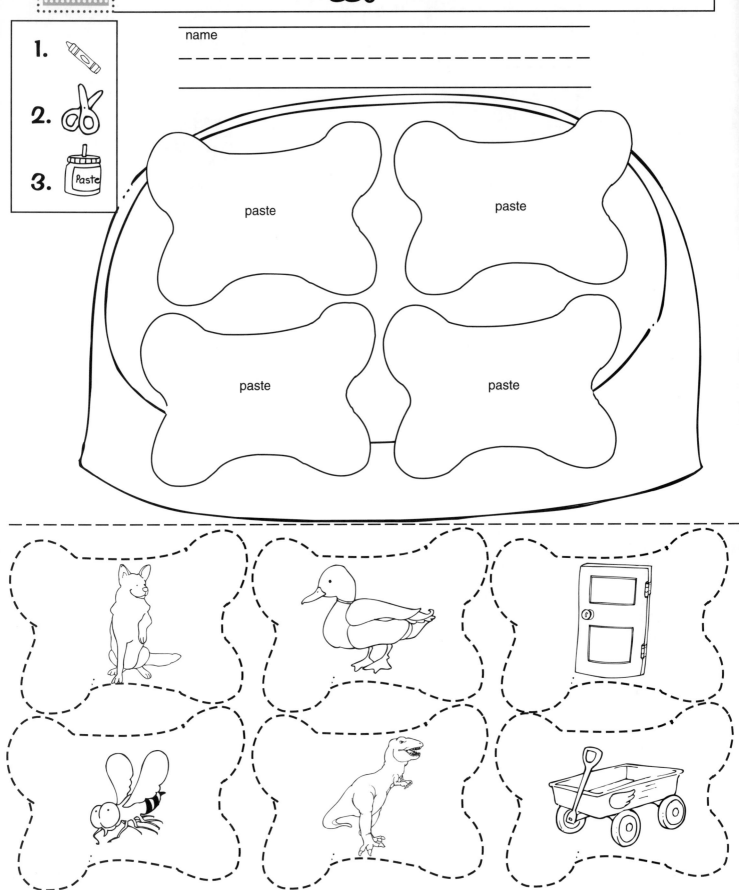

paste

paste

paste

paste

44

Fun with the Alphabet EMC 774

Dig, dog, dig.

Dig, dog, dig.

①

The Dog

Dd

fold 1

fold 2

④

②

Dig it deep. Dig it wide.

③

Drop the bone safe inside.

Dig, dog, dig.

Dig, dog, dig.

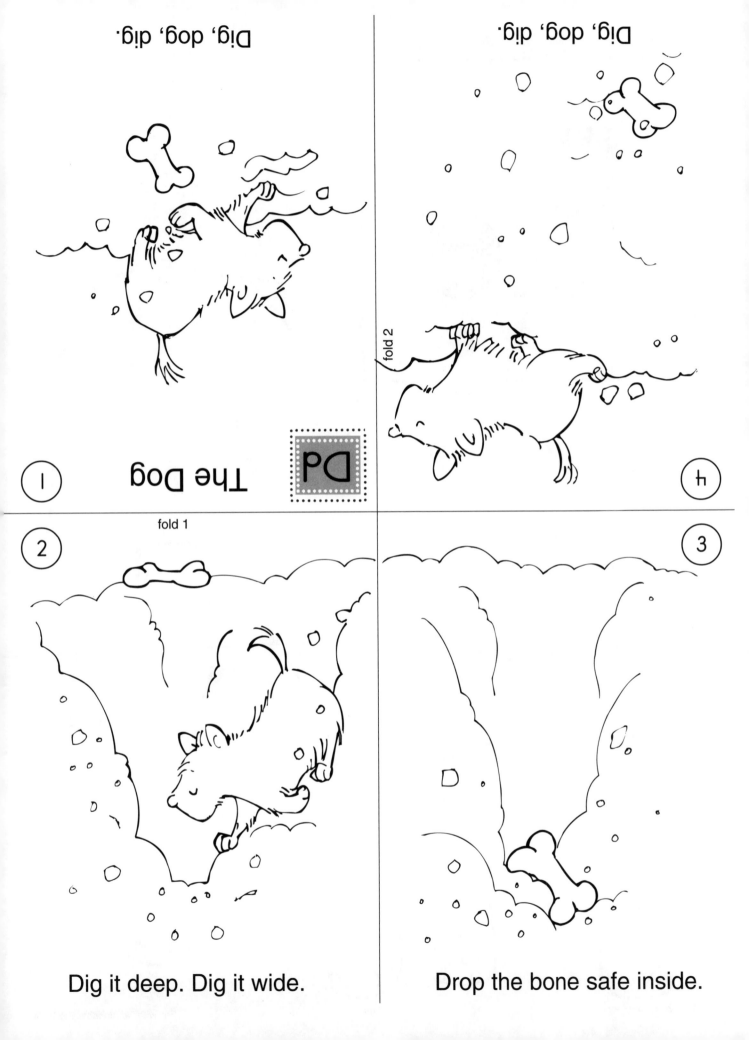

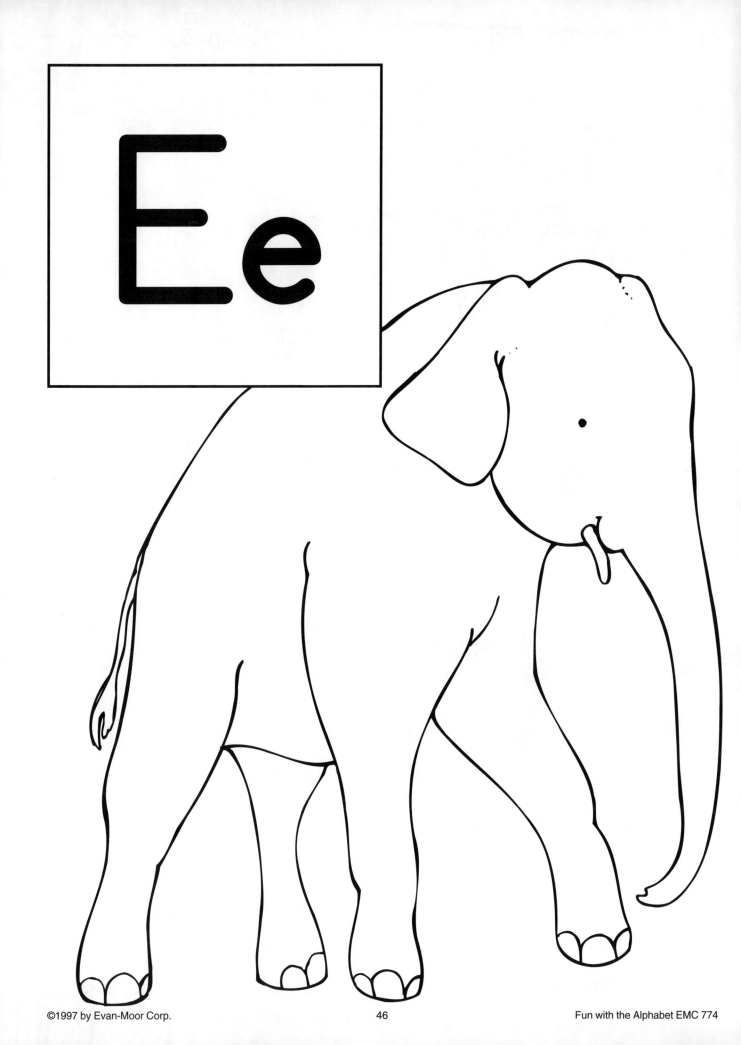

E e

46 Fun with the Alphabet EMC 774

Pages four and five provide teaching ideas for introducing and practicing each letter. Use these in conjunction with the specific resources for "E" listed below.

Have students sort objects. Put things starting with the sound "e" makes in egg cartons.

Note: Determine whether you will introduce both the short and long sounds of the vowel at the same time.

Alphabet Books

Eating the Alphabet: Fruits and Vegetables from A to Z by Lois Ehlert; Harcourt Brace, 1989.

Ed Emberley's ABC by Ed Emberly; Little, Brown, 1978

Books About Eskimos

Arctic Hunter by Diane Hoyt-Goldsmith; Holiday House, 1992. (Use illustrations of Inupiaq life in Kotzebue, Alaska.)

Eskimo Boy: LIfe in an Inupiaq Eskimo Village by Russ Kendall; Scholastic, 1992.

The Eskimo: The Inuit and Yupik People by Alice Osinski; Children's Press, 1985.

Mama, Do You Love Me? by Barbara M. Joosse; Chronicle Books, 1991.

Nunavat by Lyn Hancock; Lerner Publications, 1995. (Use appropriate pages.)

On Mother's Lap by Ann Herbert Scott; Houghton Mifflin, 1992.

Books About Eggs

Bread and Jam for Frances by Russell Hoban; Harper & Row, 1964.

Egg by Robert Burton; Dorling Kindersley, 1994.

Egg (First Discovery Book) by Pascale DeBourgoing; Scholastic, 1992.

Egg to Chick (Trophy I Can Read Book) by Millicent E. Selsam; HarperCollins, 1987.

Fiona Raps It Up by Frank Remkiewicz; Lothrop, Lee & Shephard, 1995.

Horton Hatches the Egg by Dr. Seuss; Random House, 1940.

A Nest Full of Eggs by Priscilla Belz Jenkins; HarperCollins, 1995.

Discussion: Why do you think these ice cream bars are called Eskimo Pies?

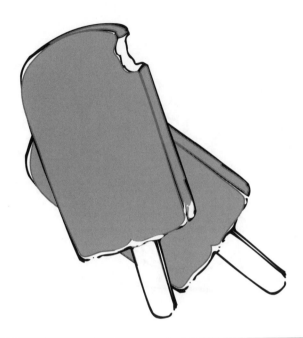

 Draw It!   **Eggs**

Direct students to fold a blank piece of paper into four sections. Draw on the chalkboard and use oral instructions to guide students to draw the following:

1. Make a small blue robin's egg.

2. Make a large brown chicken's egg.

3. Make a chicken's egg with a crack.

4. Make a hard-boiled egg with a yellow yolk.

Oral Language Experience:

Students dictate a sentence or short story about one of the pictures to an adult.

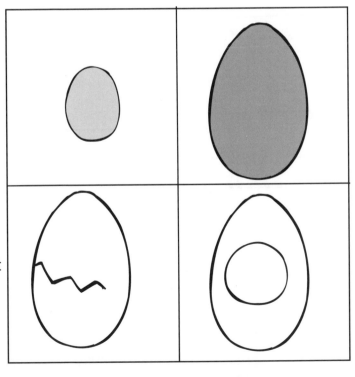

Fun with the Alphabet EMC 774

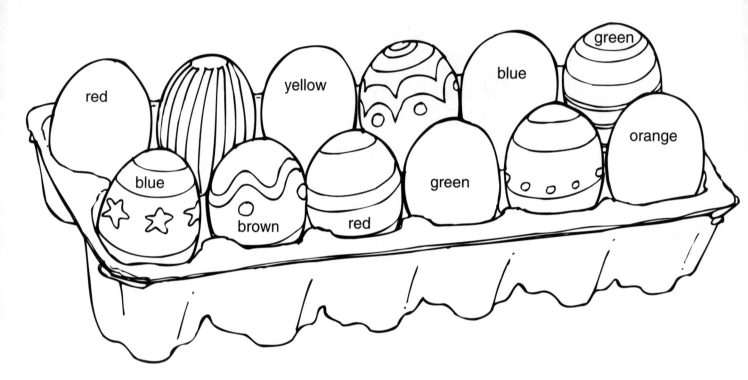

red

yellow

blue

green

blue

brown

red

green

orange

Trace and write.

e e e e e e

E E E E E

egg

 **Make It!** | # Ed the Elephant | Ee

Make Ed and his relatives to form a line of delightful elephants.

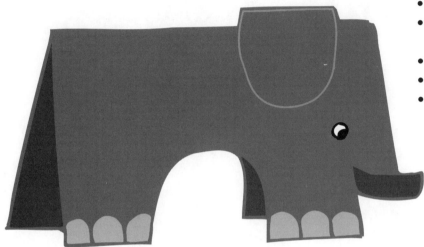

Materials:

- reproducible pattern on page 52
- grey or light brown construction paper - 9" x 12" (23 x 30.5 cm)
- scissors
- crayons
- paste

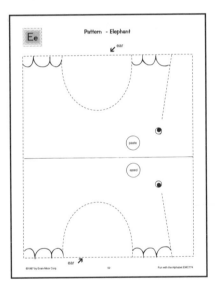

Steps to follow:

1. Cut out the patterns. Color the eyes and toenails with a crayon.

2. Fold the elephant in half along the fold line.

3. Cut out the ears. Paste where marked on the elephant.

4. Cut along the trunk line, Paste the tip of the trunk pieces together. Fold up the end of the trunk.

Pattern - Elephant

ear

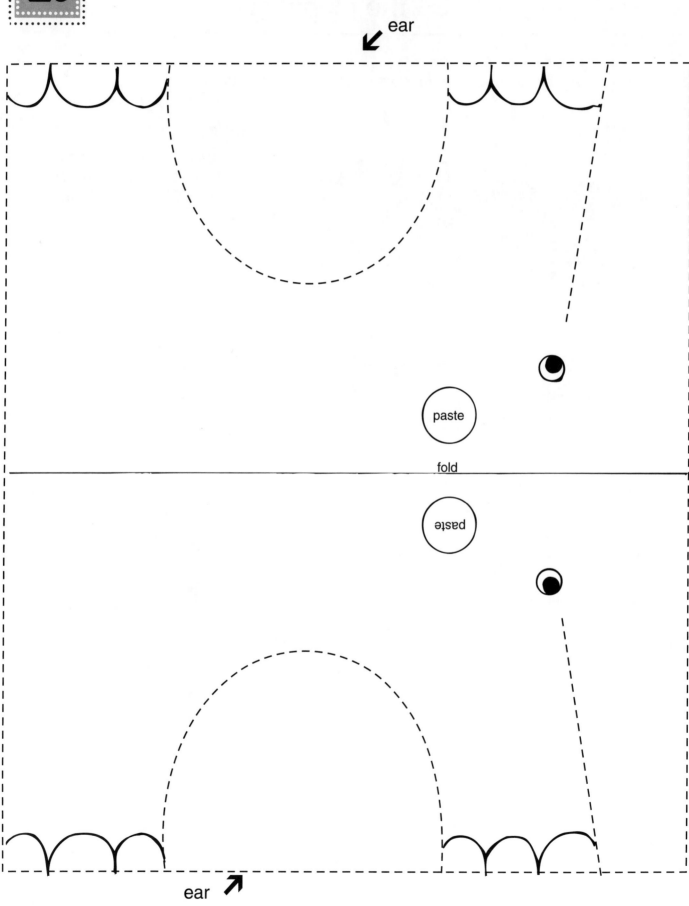

paste

paste

fold

ear

Can you find these pictures?

Fun with the Alphabet EMC 774

On the Elevator

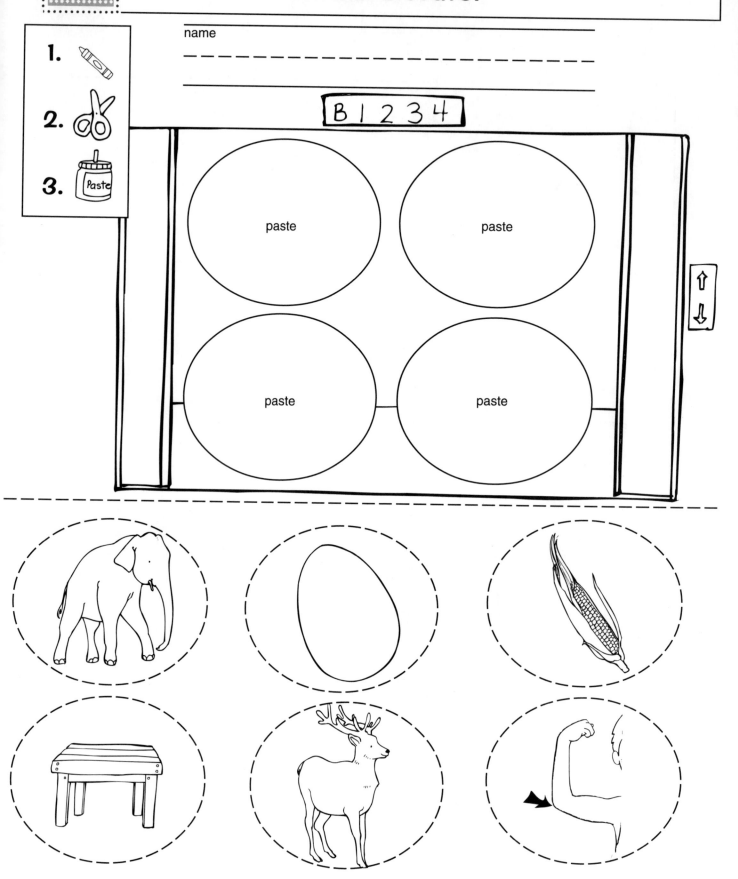

1.
2.
3. Paste

name

B 1 2 3 4

paste   paste

paste   paste

54

Fun with the Alphabet EMC 774

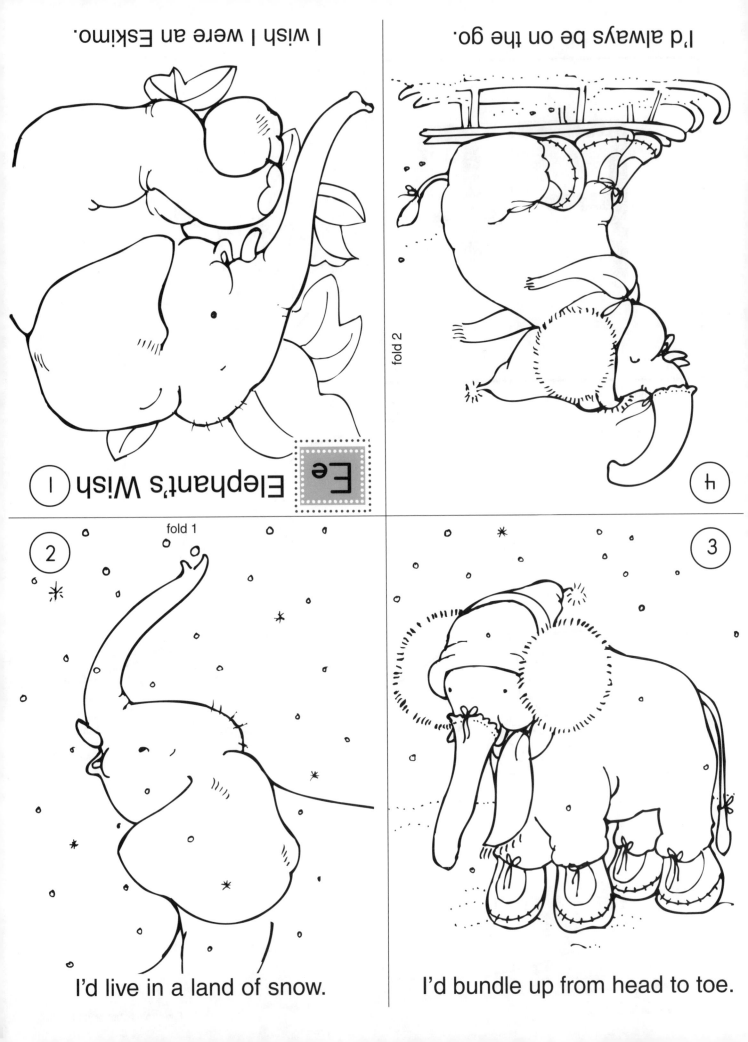

I wish I were an Eskimo.

① Elephant's Wish

Ee

I'd always be on the go.

fold 2

4

fold 1

2

I'd live in a land of snow.

3

I'd bundle up from head to toe.

F f

Fun with the Alphabet EMC 774

Pages four and five provide teaching ideas for introducing and practicing each letter. Use these in conjunction with the specific resources for "F" listed below.

Bibliography

 Read It!

Alphabet Books

From Letter to Letter by Teri Sloat; E. P. Dutton, 1989.
The Frog Alphabet Book...And Other Awesome Amphibians by Jerry Pallotta; Charlesbridge, 1990

Books About Frogs:

A Frog's Body by Joanna Cole; Morrow Junior, 1980.
Amazing Frogs & Toads (Eyewitness Junior) by Barry Clarke; Knopf, 1990.
April Showers by George Shannon; Greenwillow Books, 1995.
Frog by Steven Savage; Thomson Learning, 1995.
Frog and Toad Are Friends by Arnold Lobel; HarperCollins, 1970.
Froggy Learn to Swim by Jonathan London; Viking Children's Press, 1995.
Frogs and Toads and Tadpoles Too (Rookie Read-About Science Series) by Allan Fowler; Children's Press, 1992.
Frog, Where Are You? by Mercer Mayer; Dial Books for Young Readers, 1969.
Hurry Home, Hungry Frog by Carla Dijs; Simon & Schuster, 1995.
Jump, Frog, Jump! by Robert Kalan; Greenwillow Books, 1995 (Reissue).
That's Philomena! by Catherine Bancroft & Hannah Coale; Simon & Schuster, 1995.

Books About Feathers:

Feathers by Ruth Gordon; Simon & Schuster, 1993.
Feathers by Dorothy Marshall-Noke; Windswept House, 1990.
Feathers for Lunch by Lois Ehlart; Harcourt Brace Jovanovich, 1990.
Feathers Like a Rainbow: An Amazon Indian Tale by Flora; HarperCollins, 1989.
Feathery Animals by Angela Wilkes; Dorling Kindersley, 1992.

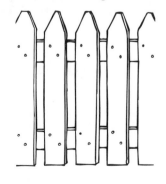

 **Eat It!**

Fortune Cookies

- 2 large eggs
- 1/2 cup (100 gm) sugar
- 4 tbs. (60 ml) vegetable oil
- 1/2 cup (63 gm) cornstarch
- 2 tbs. water (30 ml) (add a little more if the mixture is too thick.)

1. Beat eggs slightly, then add the sugar and beat until smooth.

2. Add oil and mix well.

3. Add a little of this mixture to the cornstarch. Stir until smooth. Add this to the rest of the mixture. Mix well.

4. Drop by teaspoon onto a hot griddle. Spread to a 3" (7.5 cm) circle. Brown on both sides.

5. While the cookie is still warm, place a fortune on a slip of paper in the center of the cookie and fold.

 Draw It!   **Feathers**

Direct students to fold a blank piece of paper into four sections. Draw on the chalkboard and use oral instructions to guide students to draw the following:

1. Make a fluffy blue feather.
2. Make a big feather and a small one.
3. Make a brown feather with a black tip.
4. Make a feather in a hat.

Oral Language Experience:

Students dictate a sentence or short story about one of the pictures to an adult.

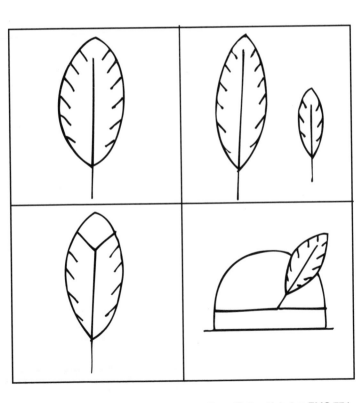

Ff

name

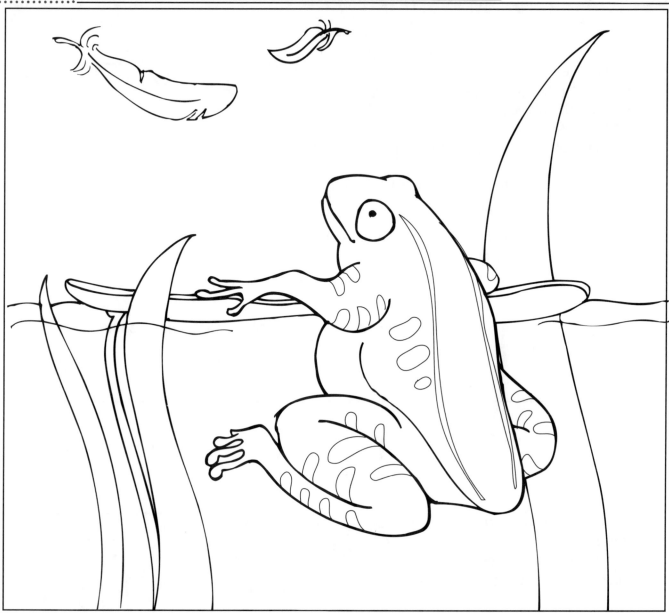

Trace and write.

f f f f f f

F F F F F

frog feather

60 Fun with the Alphabet EMC 774

Materials:

- reproducible patterns (pages 62 and 63)
- green paper.
- paper fasteners
- construction paper:
  - 2- 1 1/2" (4 cm) white squares
  - 2- 1" (2.5 cm) black squares
- scissors
- paste
- crayons

Optional:

thin strips of red paper for tongues

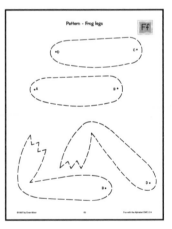

Steps to follow:

1. Cut out the body and leg patterns. Remind students to cut along the inside arm lines so that the arms can be bent in various positions.

2. Use paper fasteners to attach the legs to the body. Attach A to A, B to B, etc. The feet sections may be turned over so that the toes point in or out. Arms can be bent up.

3. Make the eyes:

   Round the black and white squares into circles.

   Paste the white circles to the frog.

   Paste the black circles inside the white circles.

4. Use a black crayon to trace the mouth and nose. A thin strip of red paper can be used to make a long tongue.

Hint:

These funny frogs can be used to make a charming bulletin board: Start with a blue background. Draw the water line with marking pen. Cut out large green lily pads and staple to the board. Put frogs on the lilypads, in the water, etc.

Pattern - Frog Legs

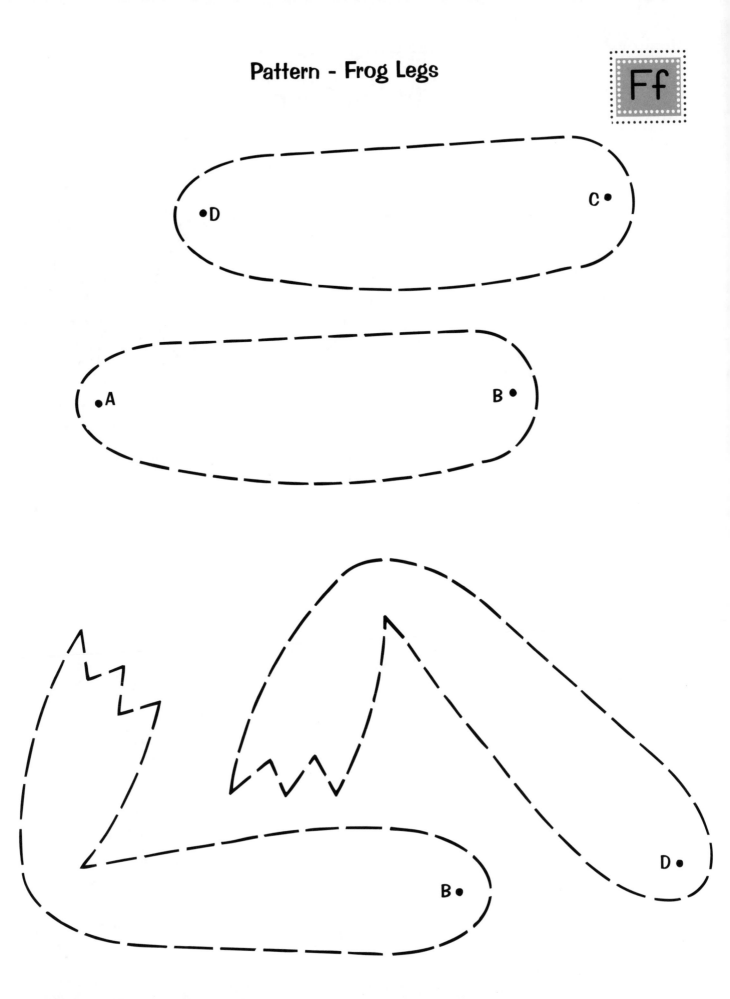

Ff

In the Pond

name

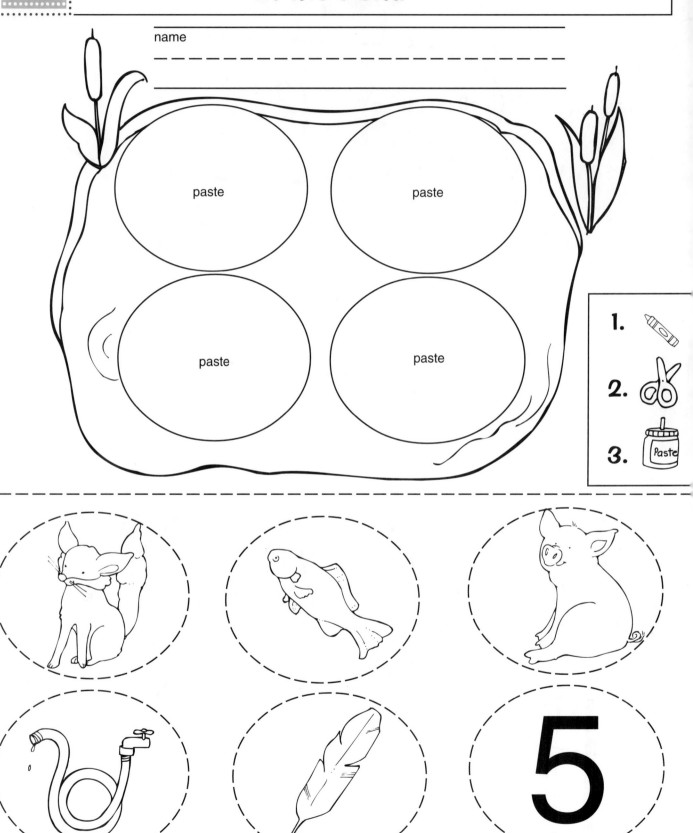

paste   paste

paste   paste

1.
2.
3. Paste

5

64   Fun with the Alphabet EMC 774

Frog hop

Frog

Ff

Kerplop!

fold 2

① ④ ② ③

fold 1

on top.

Kerplop!

Frog stop.

66

Pages four and five provide teaching ideas for introducing and practicing each letter. Use these in conjunction with the specific resources for "G" listed below.

Have students sort objects. Put things starting with the sound "g" makes in a gift box.

Alphabet Books:

A Is for Africa by Ifeoma Onyefulu; Dutton, 1973.

Jambo Means Hello: Swahili Alphabet Book by Muriel Feelings; Dial Press, 1974.

A Walk in the Rainforest by Kristin J. Pratt; Dawn Publishing, 1992.

Books About Gorillas:

Gorilla by Anthony Brown; Knopf, 1985.

Gorilla (Eyewitness book) by Ian Redmond; Knopf, 1995.

Gorilla Did It by Barbara Hazen; Simon & Schuster, 1988.

Koko's Kitten by Francine Patterson; Scholastic, 1987.

Koko's Story by Francine Patterson; Scholastic, 1989.

Raising Gordy Gorilla at the San Diego Zoo by Georgeanne Irvine; Simon & Schuster, 1990.

Books About Gifts:

Algo especial para mi (Something Special for Me in Spanish**)** translated by Aida E. Marcuse; Greenwillow Books, 1995.

The Gifts of Wali Dad: A Tale of India & Pakistan by Aaron Shepard; Atheneum, 1995.

Wibbly Pig Opens His Presents by Mick Inkpen; Artists & Writers Guild Books, 1995.

Mr. McGraw's Emporium by Jim Aylesworth; Henry Holt & Company, 1995.

Santa Through the Window by Taro Gomi; The Millbrook Press, 1995.

g

- 1/2 cup (118 ml) consomme
- 1/2 cup (118 ml) tomato juice
- 1 each (chopped:
- cucumber
- tomato
- green pepper
- 1/4 chopped small onion (optional)
- 1 tbs. (15 ml) vegetable oil
- 1 /2 tsp. (2 gm) salt

1. Mix all ingredients.

2. Chill and serve.

Serves 4-6

Serve graham crackers and grapes to less daring students.

 Draw It!   **The Gift**

Direct students to fold a blank piece of paper into four sections. Draw on the chalkboard and use oral instructions to guide students to draw the following:

1. Make a surprise gift with a red bow.

2. Make a big gift with a blue bow.

3. Make a gift with pretty polka dots.

4. Make a surprise gift. Make it colorful.

Oral Language Experience:

Students dictate a sentence or short story about one of the pictures to an adult.

1 ·   12 ·

· 11
· 10

2 ·
3 ·

4 ·   5 ·   · 9
· 8

6 ·   · 7

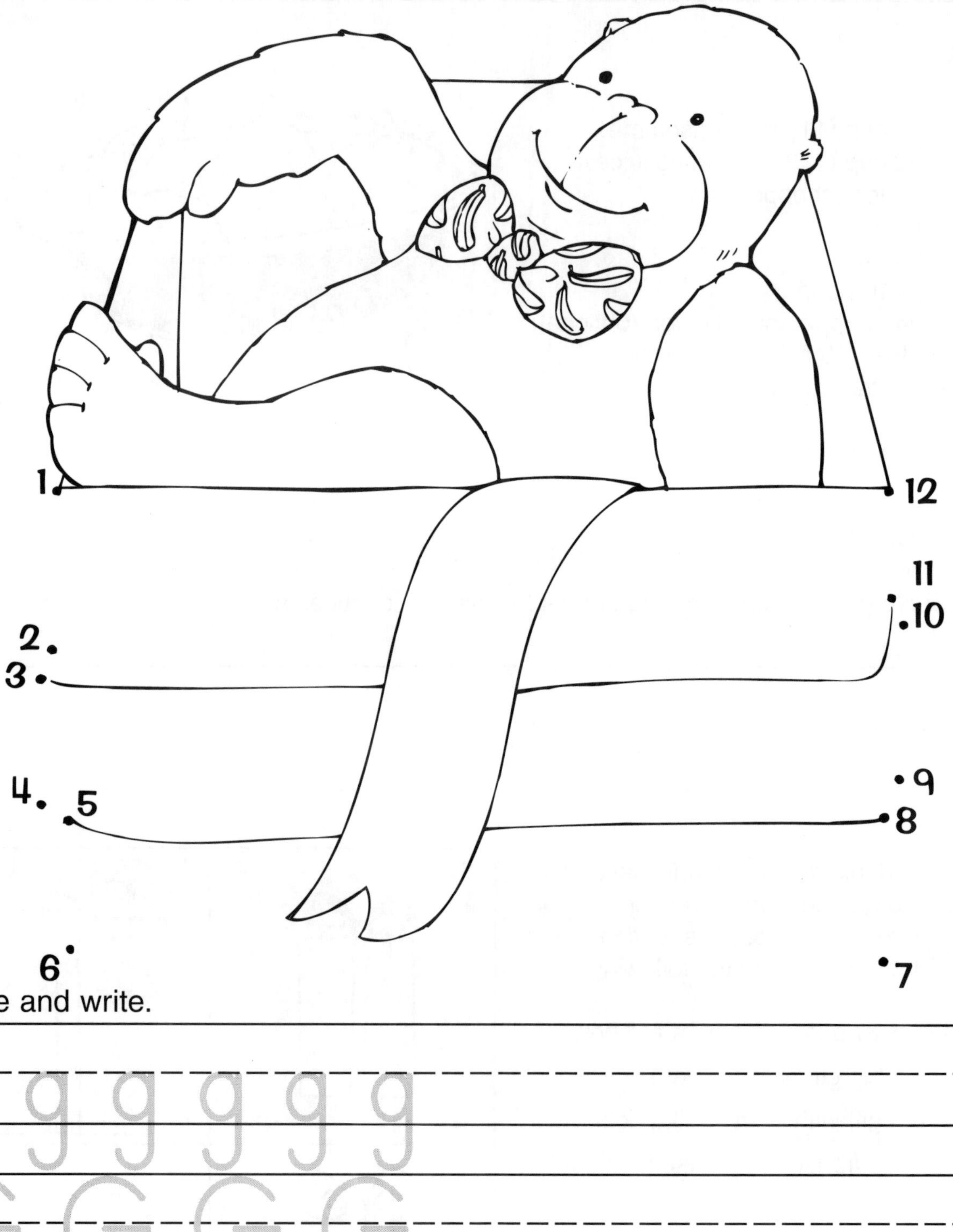

Trace and write.

g g g g g g

G G G G

gorilla gift

Grinning Gorilla

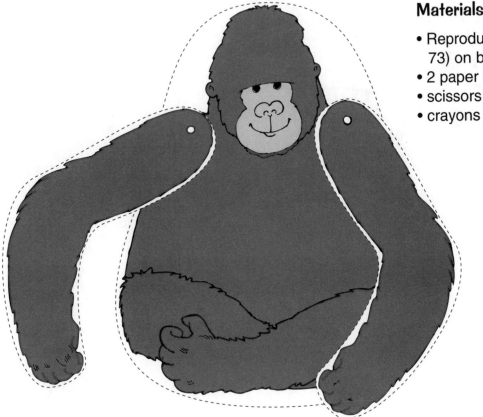

Materials:

- Reproduce the patterns (pages 72 and 73) on brown paper.
- 2 paper fasteners
- scissors
- crayons

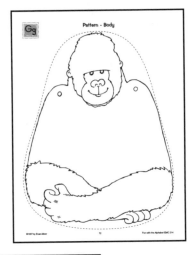

Steps to follow:

1. Cut out the gorilla parts.
2. Outline the hair, face, and feet with black crayon.
3. Attach the gorilla's arms with paper fasteners.

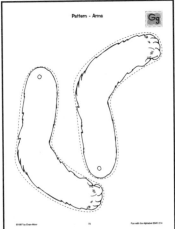

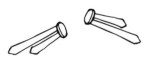

Fun with the Alphabet EMC 774

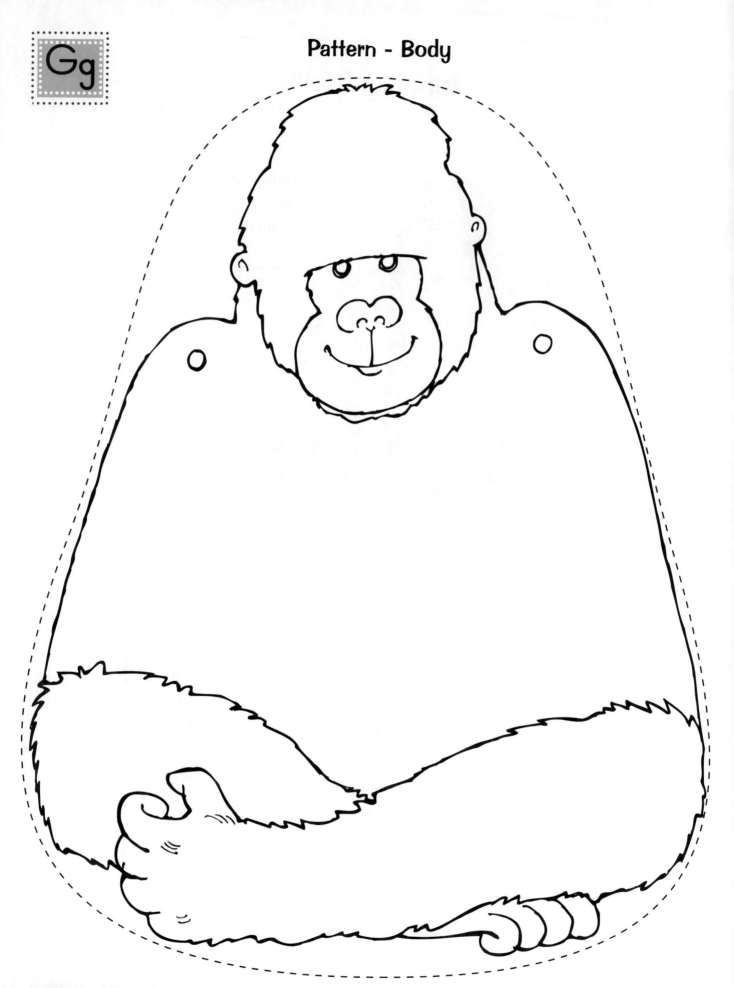

Gg

Pattern - Body

Fun with the Alphabet EMC 774

Pattern - Arms

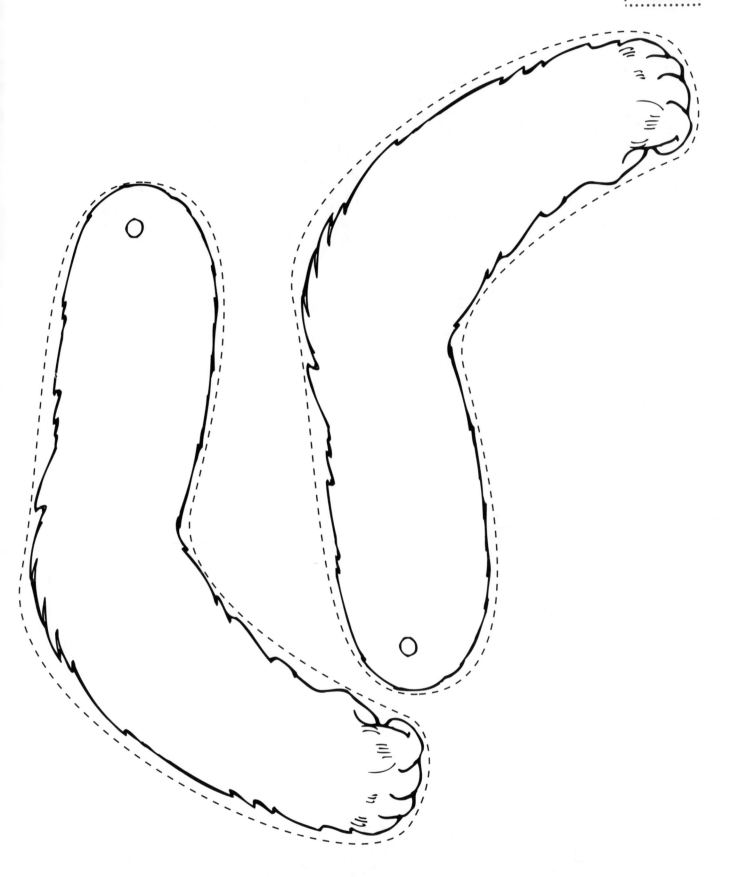

Fun with the Alphabet EMC 774

In the Gift Box

1.
2.
3.

name

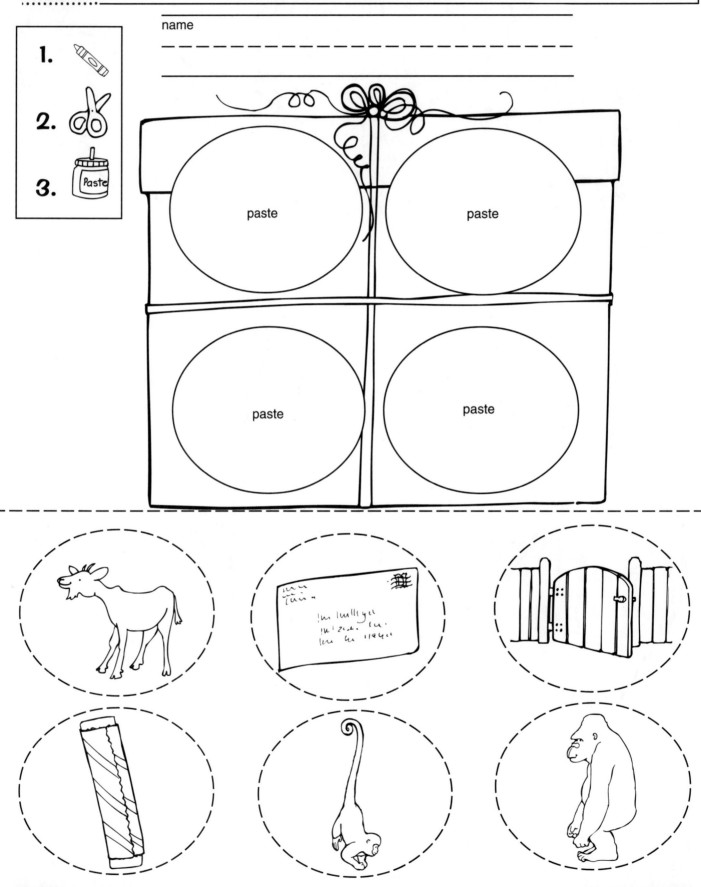

paste

paste

paste

paste

74

Fun with the Alphabet EMC 774

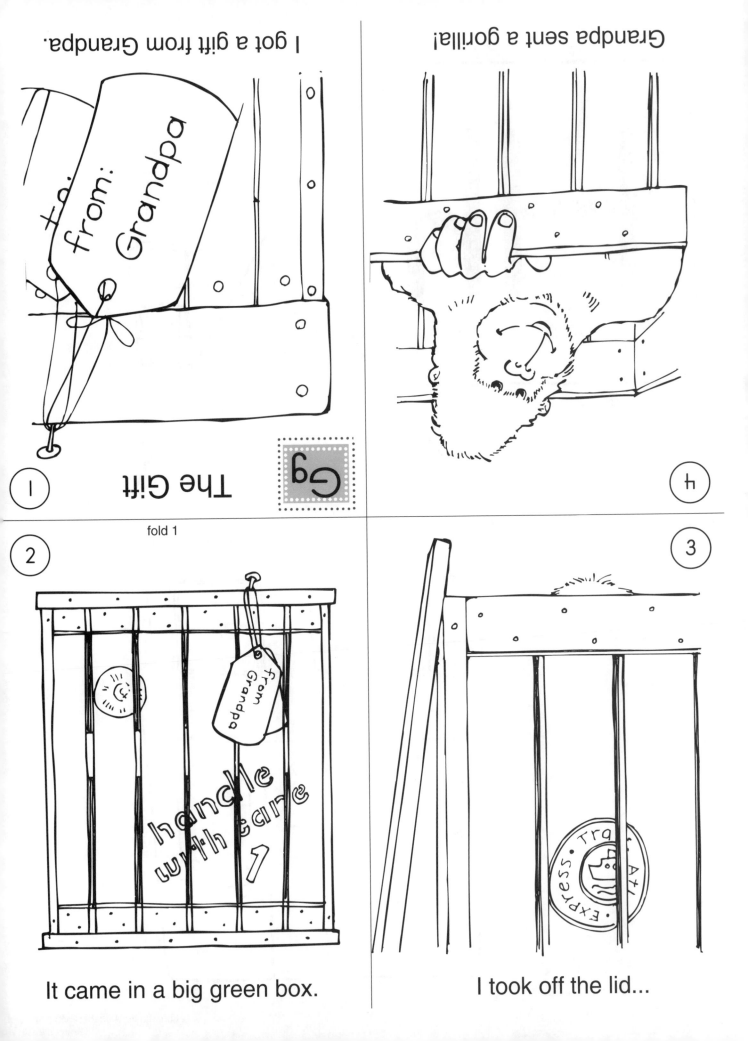

The Gift

1 I got a gift from Grandpa.

Gg

fold 1

2 It came in a big green box.

handle with care 1

from Grandpa

3 I took off the lid...

Express · Trans Atl

4 Grandpa sent a gorilla!

76

Fun with the Alphabet EMC 774

Teaching the Letter

Pages four and five provide teaching ideas for introducing and practicing each letter.
Use these in conjunction with the specific resources for "H" listed below.

Have students sort objects. Put things starting with the sound "h" makes in a hat.

Alphabet Books:

Helen Oxenbury's ABC of Things; Delacorte Press, 1971.

Chicka Chicka ABC by Bill Martin, Jr.; Simon & Schuster, 1993.

Books About Hamburgers and Other "H" Things:

George and Martha by James Marshall; Houghton Mifflin, 1972.

A Hat for Minerva Louise by Janet Stoeke; Dutton, 1994.

Hamster by Barrie Watts; Silver Burdett, 1991.

Hamsters (First Pet Series) by Kate Petty; Baron, 1993.

The Happy Hippopotami! by Bill Martin; Harcourt Brace, 1991.

Harry Takes a Bath by Harriet Zeifert; Puffin, 1993.

Horse in Harry's Room (Trophy Early I Can Read Book) by Syd Hoff; HarperCollins, 1985.

A House Is a House For Me by Mary Ann Hoberman; Viking, 1978.

House and Homes by Ann Morris; Lothrop, Lee & Shephard, 1992.

Jennie's Hat by Ezra Jack Keats; Harper & Row, 1966.

Lucille by Arnold Lobel; Harper & Row, 1964.

There's a Hippopotamus Under My Bed by Mike Thaler; Avon, 1978.

There's No Place Like Home by Marc Brown; Parents, 1984.

Spaceburger by Daniel Pinkwater; Simon & Schuster, 1993.

Read a Recipe:

Share a recipe for making hamburgers from a cookbook for children. (For example: **Boys and Girls Cookbook** published by Ideals Publishing Company has a recipe for "Fiesta Burgers" on page 15.) Write the recipe on a chart and read it together as you would a poem or a chant. If you are feeling brave, bring in all of the necessary equipment and cook hamburgers with your class.

Books About Hills:

The Little House by Virginia Lee Burton; Houghton Mifflin, 1978 (The little house sits on a hill.)

The Grand Old Duke of York by Maureen Raffey; Whispering Coyote Press, 1993. (The duke marches his men up and down a hill.)

How Mountains Are Made by Kathleen Weidner Zoehfeld; HarperCollins, 1995.

Mountains by Seymour Simon; Morrow Junior Books, 1994.

Hot dog

- 4 round pieces of zucchini or carrot for wheels
- 4 raisins for hubcaps
- 2 toothpicks

Taste honeycomb as an extra "h" treat

 **Draw It!**　　**The Hill**

Direct students to fold a blank piece of paper into four sections. Draw on the chalkboard and use oral instructions to guide students to draw the following:

1. Make a high green hill.

2. Make a little house on a hill.

3. Make a big house on a hill.

4. Make a house on a hill on a hazy (gray) day.

Oral Language Experience:

Students dictate a sentence or short story about one of the pictures to an adult.

name

Write It!

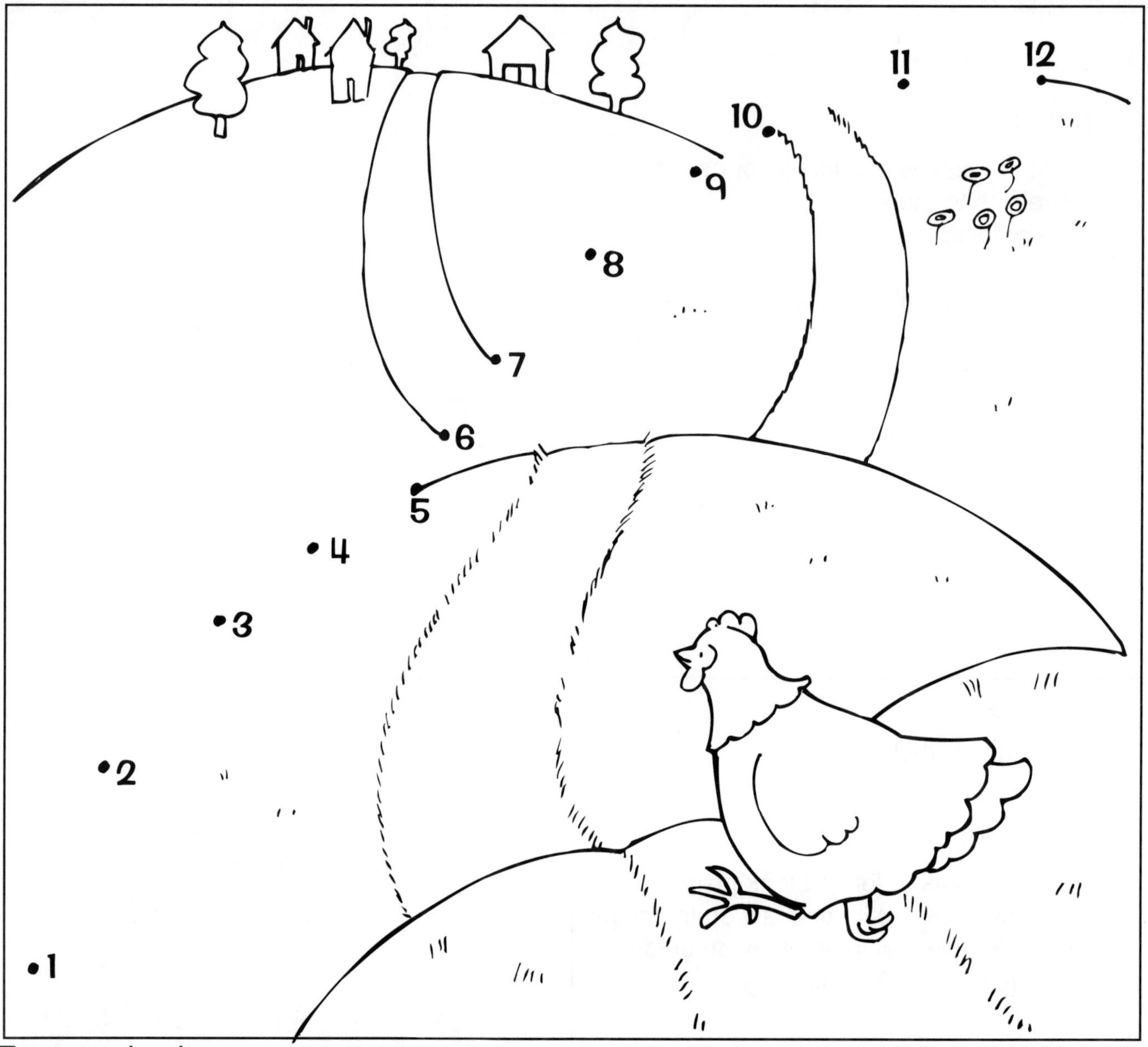

Trace and write.

h h h h h

H H H H

hill hen

Fun with the Alphabet EMC 774

Make It! A Hearty Hamburger

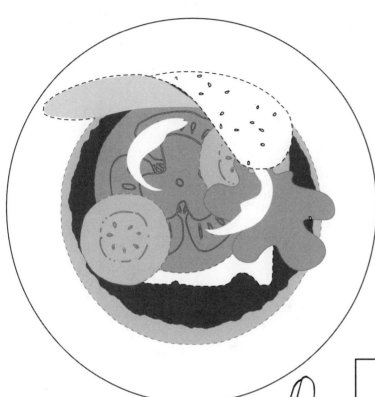

Materials:

- reproducible patterns on page 82 and 83
- light brown paper for bun
- crayons
- scissors
- paste
- construction paper scraps: green for lettuce, white for onions
- paper plates

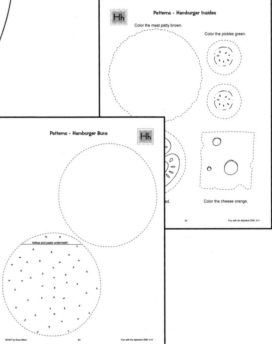

Steps to follow:

1. Cut out and color all the hamburger "insides." Cut out the hamburger bun.

2. Paste the bottom bun on a paper plate.

3. Add mustard and catsup by coloring the bun with crayons.

4. Assemble the hamburger by pasting on the inside parts.

5. Add scraps of green and white for lettuce and onion.

6. Fold the top bun on the fold line. Put paste on the fold only, so the bun can be lifted to peek inside the hamburger.

         Fun with the Alphabet EMC 774

Patterns - Hamburger Insides

Color the meat patty brown.

Color the pickles green.

Color the tomato red.

Color the cheese orange.

Fun with the Alphabet EMC 774

Patterns - Hamburger Buns

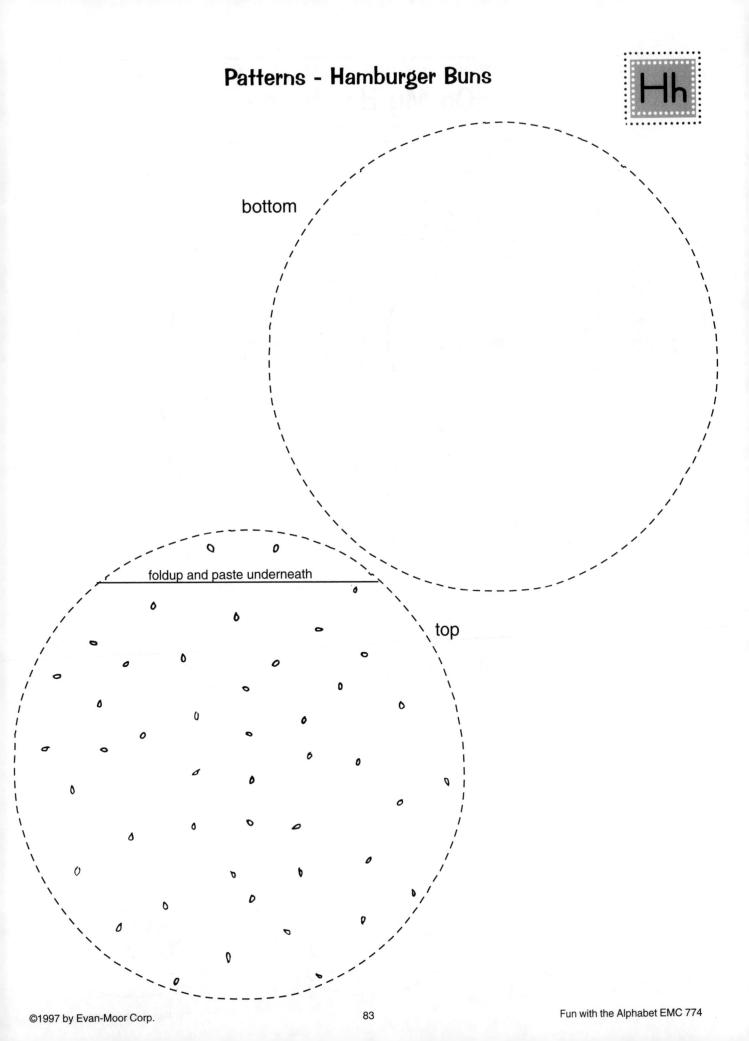

Hh

bottom

foldup and paste underneath

top

Fun with the Alphabet EMC 774

Hh

On My Hamburger

name _____

_____

1. ✏️

2. ✂️

3. Paste

paste

paste

paste

paste

Fun with the Alphabet EMC 774

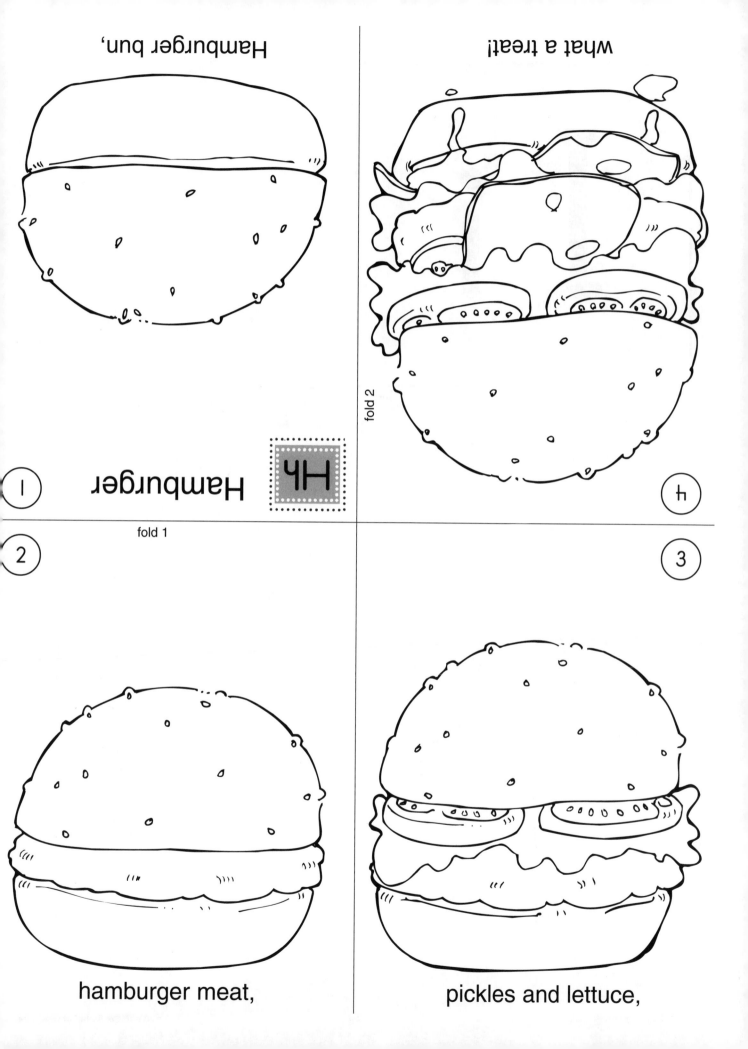

Hamburger bun,

what a treat!

Hamburger

Hh

fold 1

fold 2

1

4

2

3

hamburger meat,

pickles and lettuce,

86

Pages four and five provide teaching ideas for introducing and practicing each letter. Use these in conjunction with the specific resources for "I" listed below.

Have students sort objects. Put things starting with the sound "i" makes in an icetray.

Note: Determine whether you will introduce both the short and long sounds of the vowel at the same time.

Bibliography

 **Read It!**

Alphabet Books:

Add It, Dip It, Fix It: A Book of Verbs by R. M. Schneider; Houghton Mifflin, 1995.

Brian Wildsmith's ABC; Franklin Watts, Inc., 1962.

What's Inside? The Alphabet Book by Satoshi Kitamura; Farrar, Straus, and Giroux, 1985.

Books About Inchworms:

Inch Boy by Junko Morimoto; Puffin, 1988.

Inch by Inch by Leo Lionni; Morrow, 1994.

Inch by Inch: The Garden Song by David Mallet; HarperCollins , 1995.

Worms by Jennifer Coldrey; Bookwright Press, 1986.

Books About Igloos:

Building An Igloo by Ulli Steltzer; Henry Holt & Company, 1995.

Houses of Snow, Skin and Bones by Bonnie Shemie; Tundra Books, 1989.

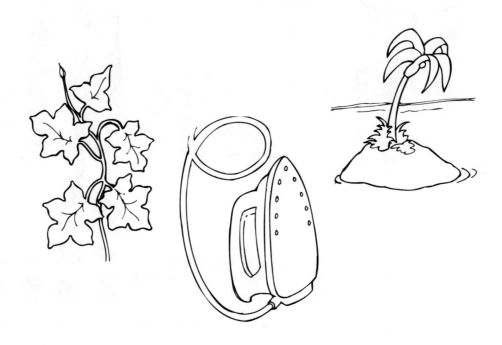

 **Eat It!**  # Icky Stickys

 I i

- 1/4 cup (57 gm) margarine
- 4 cups (200 gm) miniature marshmallows
- 5 cups (132 gm) Rice Krispies®
- Ice cream sticks

1. Melt the margarine over low heat.

2. Add marshmallows. Stir until they melt. Then cook 3-4 minutes longer, stirring constantly.

3. Remove from the burner and add the cereal. Stir until the cereal is coated.

4. Form into balls* and add an ice cream stick handle.

**This is very hot. An adult should form the balls. Butter your hands first!

Draw It! # The Igloo

Direct students to fold a blank piece of paper into four sections. Draw on the chalkboard and use oral instructions to guide students to draw the following:

1. Make an igloo made of ice.

2. Make an igloo with a fire inside.

3. Make a small igloo.

4. Make an igloo on a sunny day.

Oral Language Experience:

Students dictate a sentence or short story about one of the pictures to an adult.

 Fun with the Alphabet EMC 774

I i name

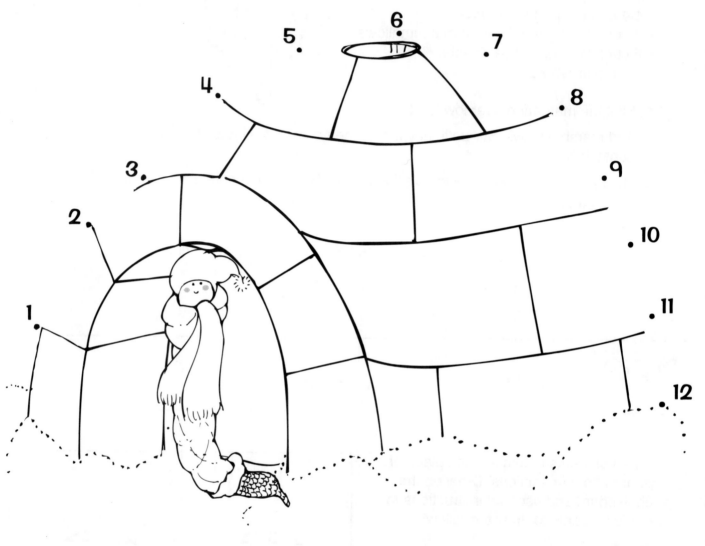

Trace and write.

igloo

Inch this little worm across the floor by pulling the string.

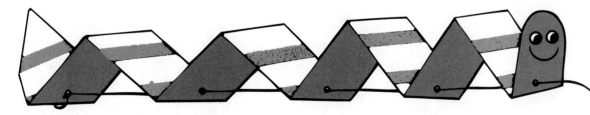

Materials:

- Reproduce page 92 on brightly-colored paper.
- 60" (152 cm) piece of yarn
- hole punch
- crayons
- scissors

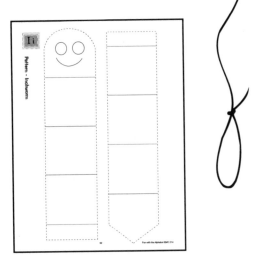

Steps to follow:

1. Cut out the inchworm pattern parts. Color in stripes.

2. Paste the two strips of construction paper together.

3. Accordion fold the strip along the fold lines.

4. Pinch the segments together and punch one hole through the worm. (An adult will need to do this step.)

5. Slip the yarn through the hole. Tie one end to the last segment of the worm. Tie a loop in the other end.

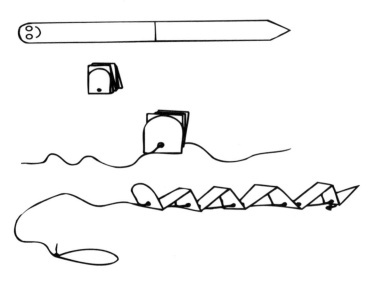

Fun with the Alphabet EMC 774

Pattern - Inchworm

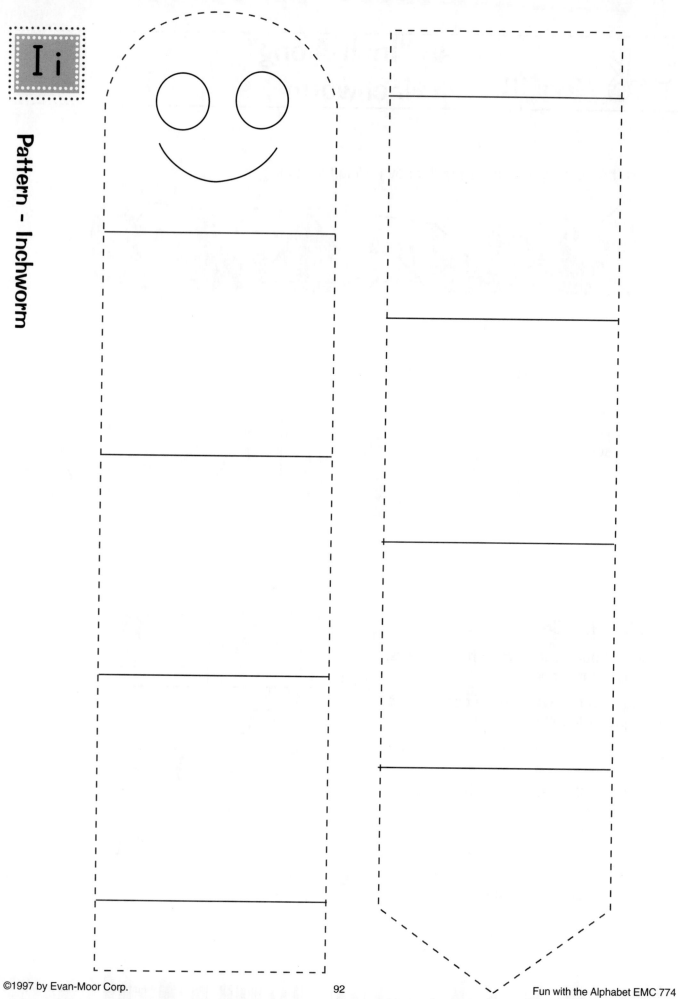

Fun with the Alphabet EMC 774

A Puzzle

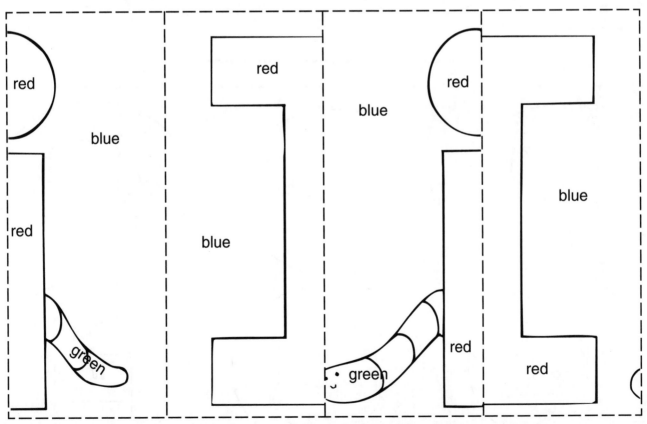

Fun with the Alphabet EMC 774

I i

In the Box

name _____

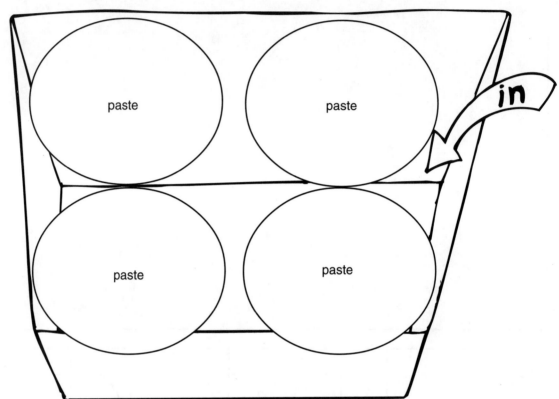

1. 🖍️
2. ✂️
3. Paste

paste   paste

paste   paste

in

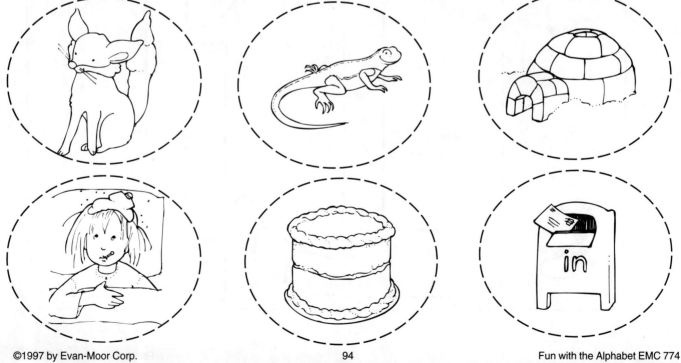

94

Fun with the Alphabet EMC 774

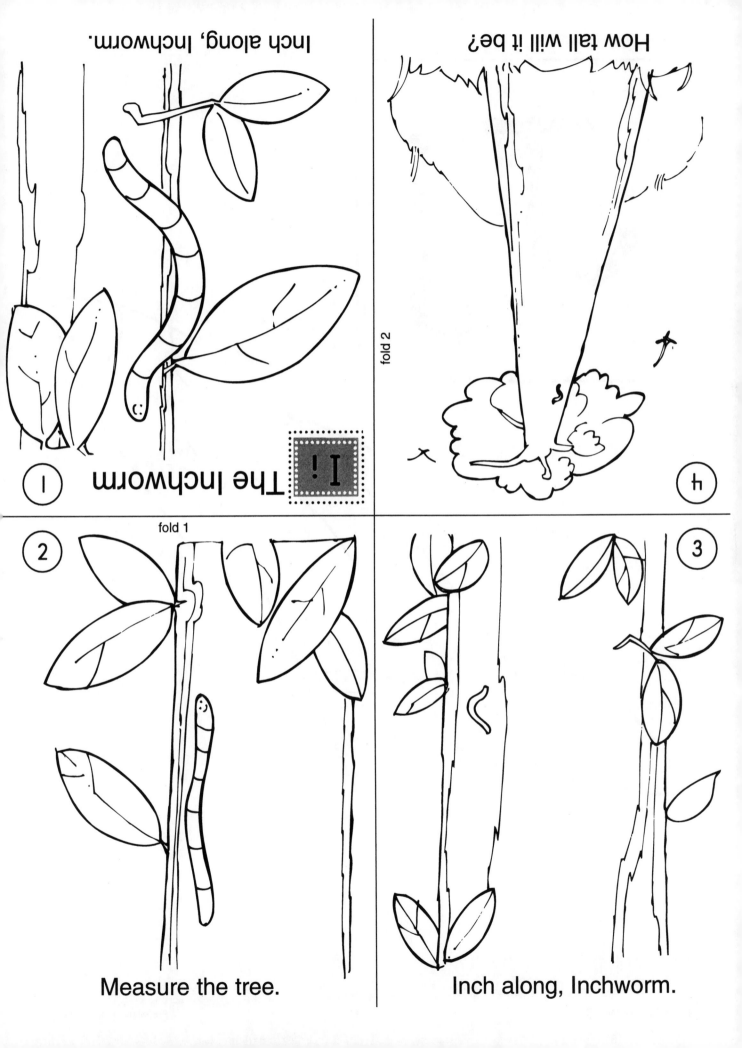

The Inchworm I i

1. Inch along, Inchworm.

2. Measure the tree.

3. Inch along, Inchworm.

4. How tall will it be?

fold 1

fold 2

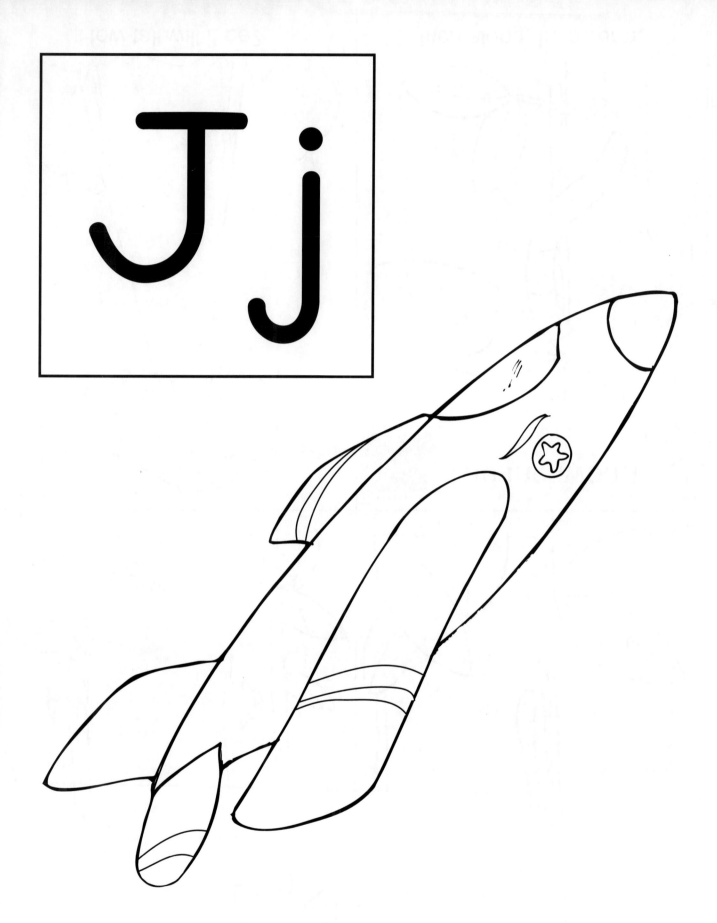

96

Fun with the Alphabet EMC 774

 **Learn It!**

Teaching the Letter

Pages four and five provide teaching ideas for introducing and practicing each letter. Use these in conjunction with the specific resources for "J" listed below.

Have students sort objects. Put things starting with the sound "j" makes inside a travel bag.

Alphabet Books:

The Ocean Alphabet Book by Jerry Pallotta; Charlesbridge, 1986.

O Is For Orca: A Pacific Northwest Alphabet Book by Andrea Helman; Sasquatch, 1995.

Under the Sea From A to Z by Anne Doubilet; Crown, 1991.

Zoomrimes: Poems About Things that Go by Sylvia Cassedy; HarperCollins, 1993.

Books About Jet Planes:

Airplane by Christopher Maynard; Dorling Kindersley, 1995.

Jetliner: From Takeoff to Touchdown by Chris Chant; Gloucester Press, 1982.

Jet Planes by Ray Broekel; Children's Press, 1987. (Use appropriate pages.)

Projects with Flight by John Williams; Gareth Stevens, 1992.

Books About Jellyfish:

Down in the Sea - the Jellyfish by Patricia Kite; Albert Whitman, 1992.

Jellyfish by Lynn Stone; Rourke, 1993. (Use appropriate pages.)

Jellyfish and Other Sea Creatures photographs by Peter Parks; Oxford Scientific Films; Putnam, 1982.

Fun with the Alphabet EMC 774

It's fun to make your gelatin in three colors (red, yellow, blue). Children can then eat a rainbow of colors. Add a whipped cream "cloud" to make it extra delicious. Have everyone wiggle their jello and watch it "jiggle" before they eat it.

 Draw It! | **The Jellies**

Direct students to fold a blank piece of paper into four sections. Draw on the chalkboard and use oral instructions to guide students to draw the following:

1. Make a red jellyfish.

2. Make a green jellyfish with red tentacles.

3. Make two jellyfish. One is red and one is green.

4. Make a surprise jellyfish.

Oral Language Experience:

Students dictate a sentence or short story about one of the pictures to an adult.

Fun with the Alphabet EMC 774

Jj

name

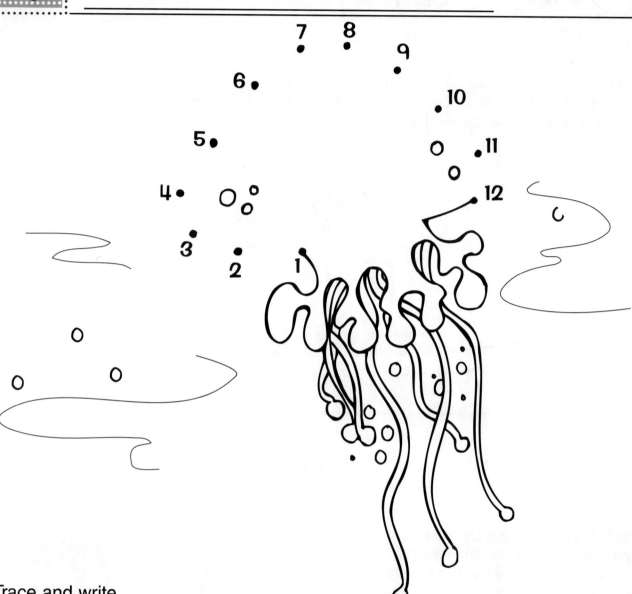

Trace and write.

jjjjjjj

JJJJJJ

jellyfish

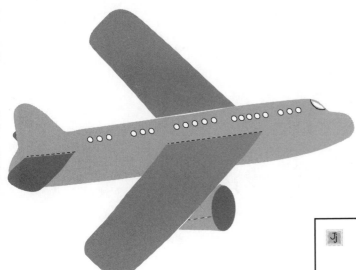

Materials:

- reproducible patterns on pages 102 and 103
- white, gray, or light blue construction paper
- scissors
- razor blade or mat knife (adult use only)
- crayons
- glue or paste

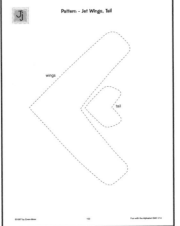

Steps to follow:

1. Decorate the jet parts with crayons. Add more windows, numbers, etc.

2. Cut out all the pattern parts.

3. Assemble the jet by slipping the wings and tail through the proper precut slits. (An adult will need to cut these slits.)

4. To make the engines:

   a. Paste each engine pattern to form a cylinder.

   b. Paste a cylinder on the underside of each wing.

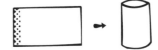

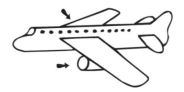

Note:

This jet is strictly kid-powered. It will not fly if thrown.

Hint:

To save time when making the jet, cut the slits for the wing and tail with a razor blade or mat knife before you give the pattern pages to the children.

Fun with the Alphabet EMC 774

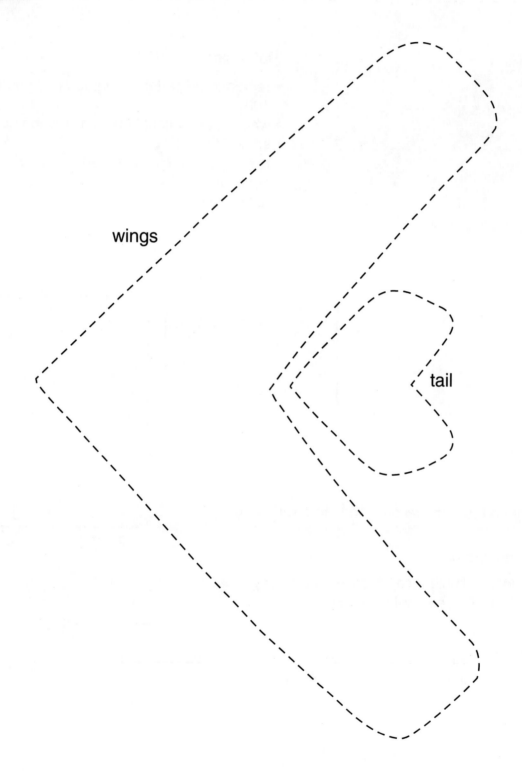

wings

tail

Fun with the Alphabet EMC 774

Pattern - Body, Engines

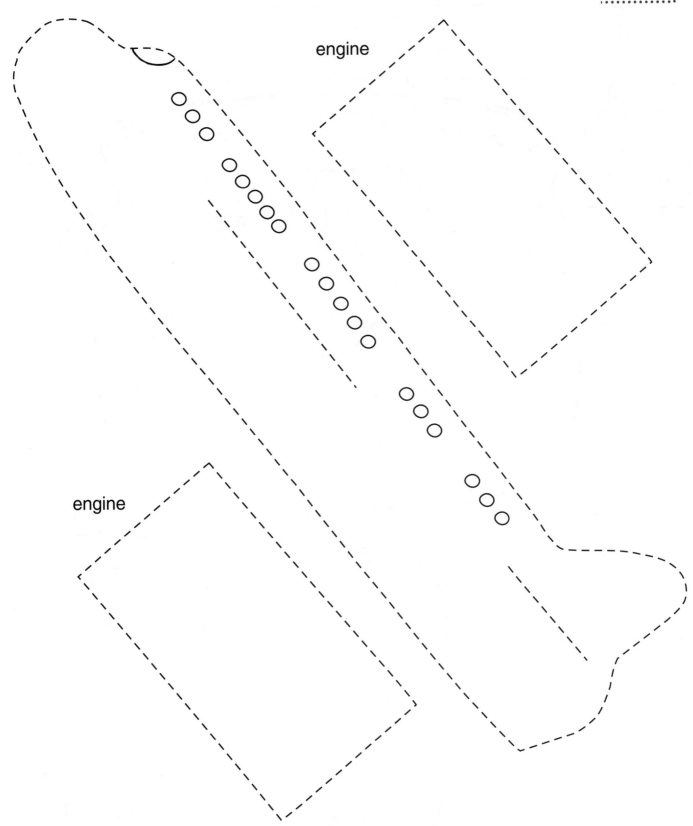

engine

engine

Fun with the Alphabet EMC 774

Fill the Jar

name

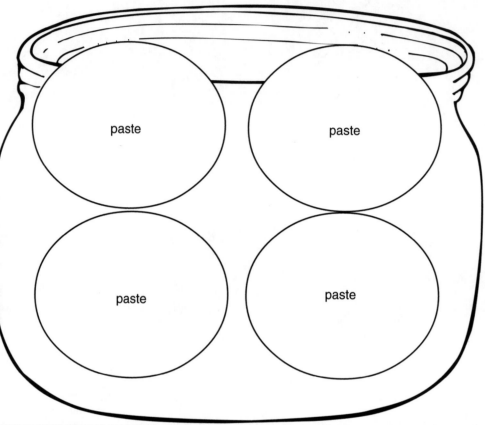

1. (crayon)

2. (scissors)

3. Paste

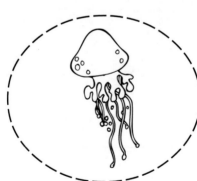

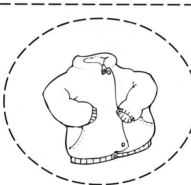

Fun with the Alphabet EMC 774

A jet is in the sky.

flying swiftly by?

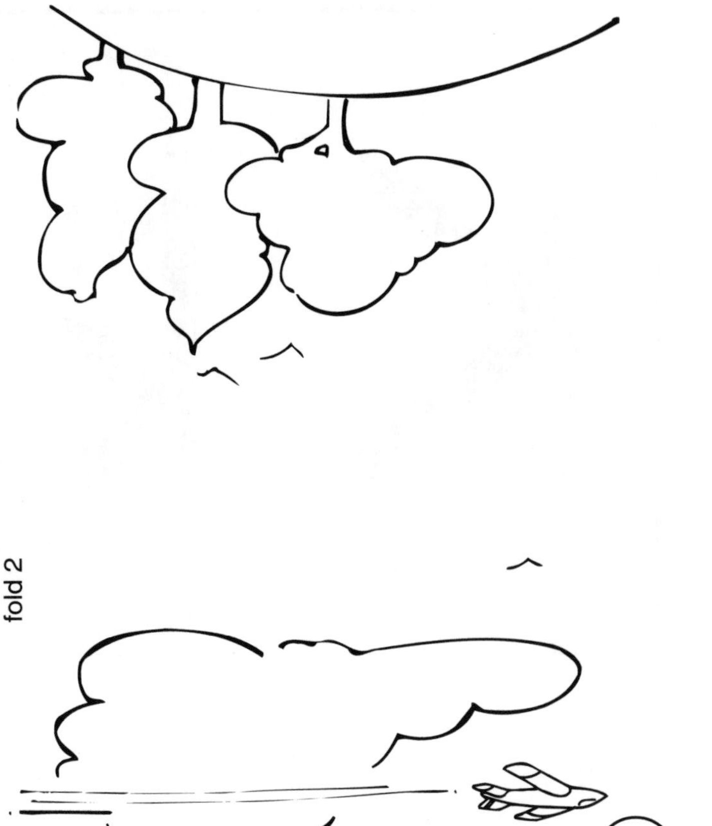

The Jet

Jj

fold 2

1

4

fold 1

2

3

A jet is in the sky.

Can you see it overhead

Teaching the Letter

Pages four and five provide teaching ideas for introducing and practicing each letter. Use these in conjunction with the specific resources for "K" listed below.

Have students sort objects. Put things starting with the sound "k" makes in a kettle.

Alphabet Books:

Anno's Alphabet by Mitsumasa Anno; Crowell, 1975.

Clifford's ABC by Norman Bridwell; Scholastic, 1983.

Kangaroo's Adventure in Alphabet Town by Janet McDonnell; Children's Press , 1992.

Books About Kangaroos:

Joey Runs Away by Jack Kent; Prentice-Hall, 1985.

Kangaroo by Paula Hogan; Raintree Steck-Vaughn, 1979.

Kangaroo by Caroline Arnold; Morrow, 1987.

Katy No-Pocket by Emmy Payne; Houghton Mifflin, 1973.

Kangaroos (Baby Animal Series) by Kate Petty; Barron, 1993.

Books About Kites:

Curious George Flies a Kite by Margaret Rey; Houghton Mifflin, 1958.

Dragon Kite by Valerie Reddix; Lothrop, Lee & Shepard, 1992.

The Kite (My First Reader Series) by Mary Packard; Childrens Press, 1990.

One Windy Day by Jane Caraway; Raintree Publishers, 1990.

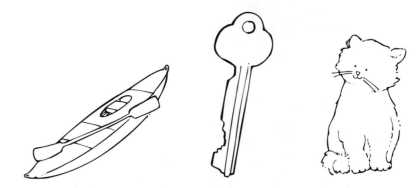

 **Eat It!** | **Kiwi Kabobs** |

1. Peel kiwi fruit.
2. Cut each kiwi into thick chunks.
3. Place the pieces on a toothpick.

If you can't find kiwis at your market, have chocolate kisses instead.

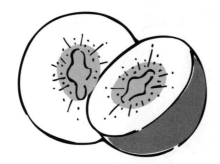

 Draw It! **The Kite**

Direct students to fold a blank piece of paper into four sections. Draw on the chalkboard and use oral instructions to guide students to draw the following:

1. Make a big orange kite.
2. Make a blue kite with a purple tail.
3. Make a big red kite and a little blue kite.
4. Make a kite with polka dots of many colors.

Oral Language Experience:

Students dictate a sentence or short story about one of the pictures to an adult.

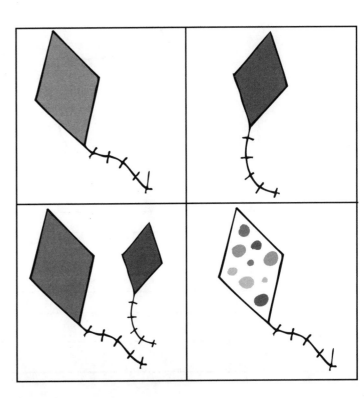

Kk

name

 **Write It!**

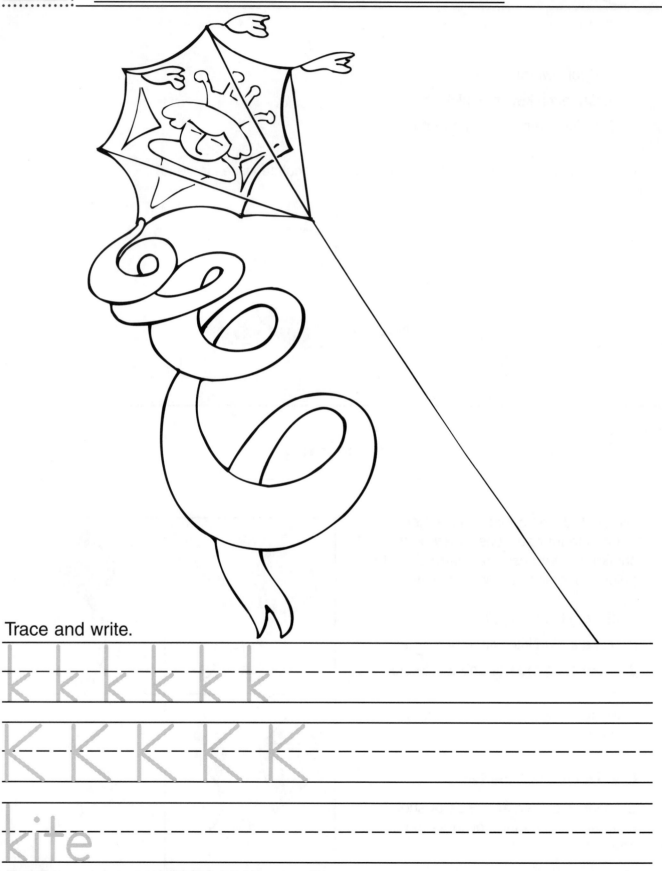

Trace and write.

k k k k k

K K K K K

kite

Materials:

- Reproduce the patterns (pages 112 and 113) on brown paper.
- scissors
- paste
- black crayon
- craft stick

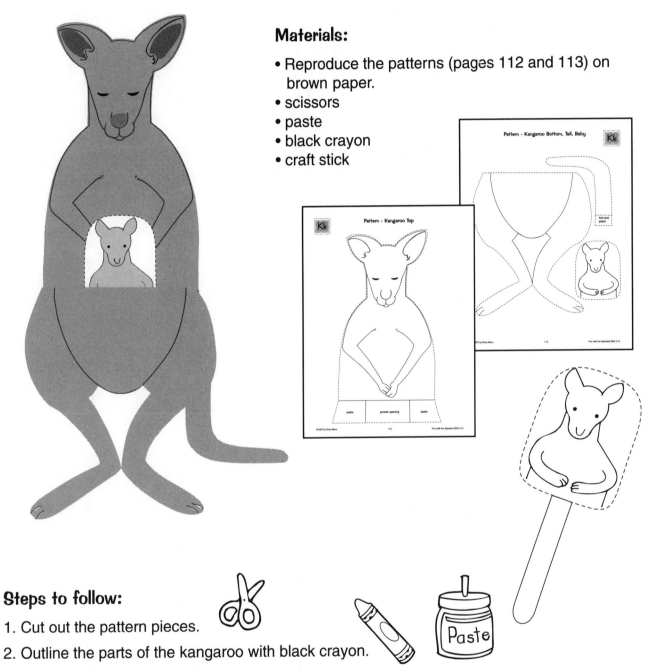

Steps to follow:

1. Cut out the pattern pieces.

2. Outline the parts of the kangaroo with black crayon.

3. Paste the lower and upper body pieces in the designated places. (Explain to students that the place with no paste makes the mother kangaroo's pocket.)

4. Attach the tail to the back of the kangaroo. Put it at an angle so that it can be seen from the front.

5. Paste the little kangaroo to an ice cream stick. Slip it through the pocket opening from the bottom. Now the baby can pop in and out of Mother's pouch.

Pattern - Kangaroo Top

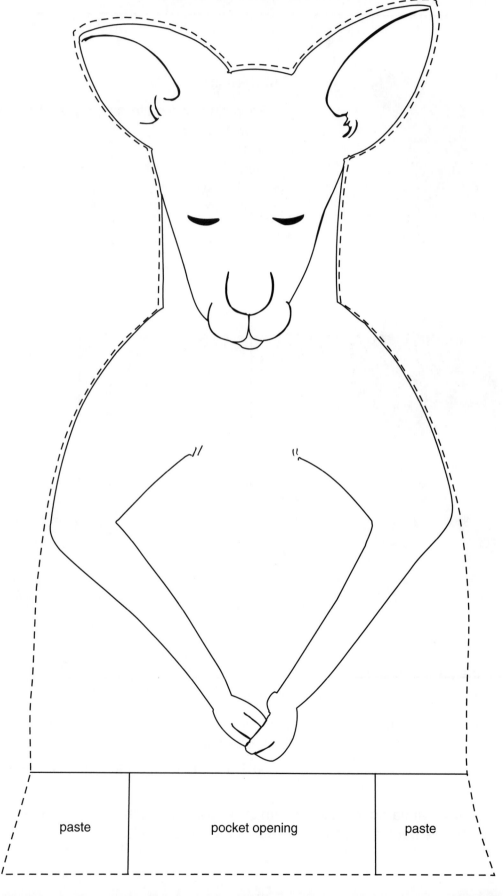

paste

pocket opening

paste

Fun with the Alphabet EMC 774

Pattern - Kangaroo Bottom, Tail, Baby

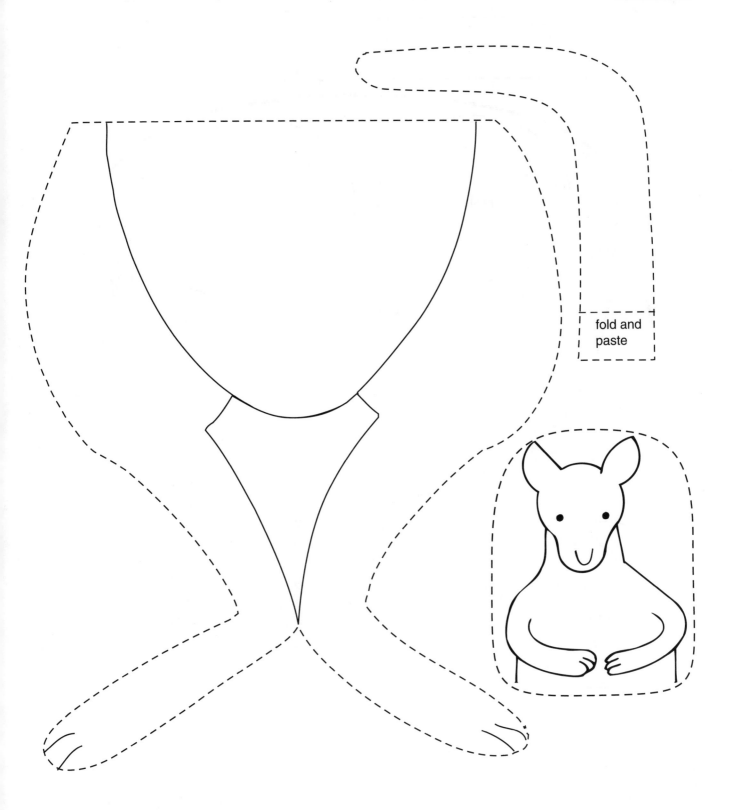

fold and paste

Fun with the Alphabet EMC 774

In the Kettle

name _____

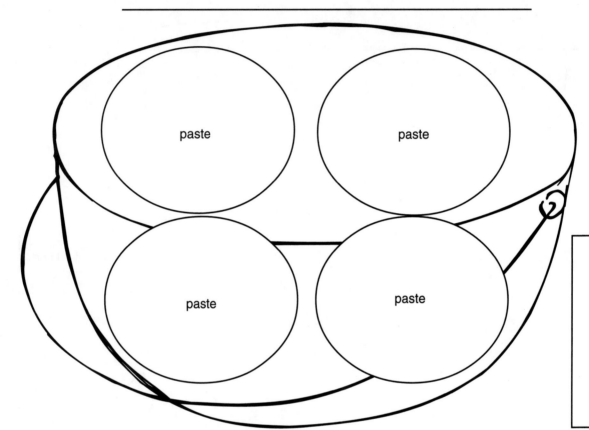

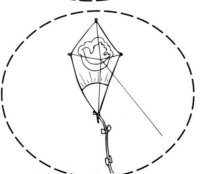

 **Make It!**

Marvelous Moose
(A Bag Puppet)

 Mm

What "m" foods could this hungry moose have for lunch?

Materials:

- reproducible patterns on pages 132 and 133
- light brown construction paper
- a brown lunch bag
- red construction paper - 3" x 6" (7.5 x 15 cm)
- scissors
- crayons

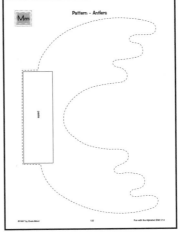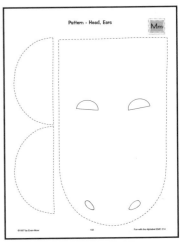

Steps to follow:

1. Cut out the pattern pieces.
2. Color eyes and nostrils with black crayon.
3. Paste the head to the paper bag.
4. Trace around the moose's nose with brown crayon to create a jaw line on the bag.
5. Round two corners of the red construction paper to make a tongue. Paste the tongue under the bag flap. Draw teeth along the jaw line.
6. Paste the antlers to the back of the bag.
7. Paste the ears behind the antlers.

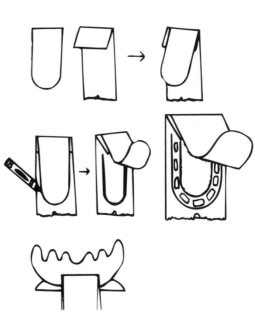

©1997 by Evan-Moor Corp. 131 Fun with the Alphabet EMC 774

Pattern - Antlers

Mm

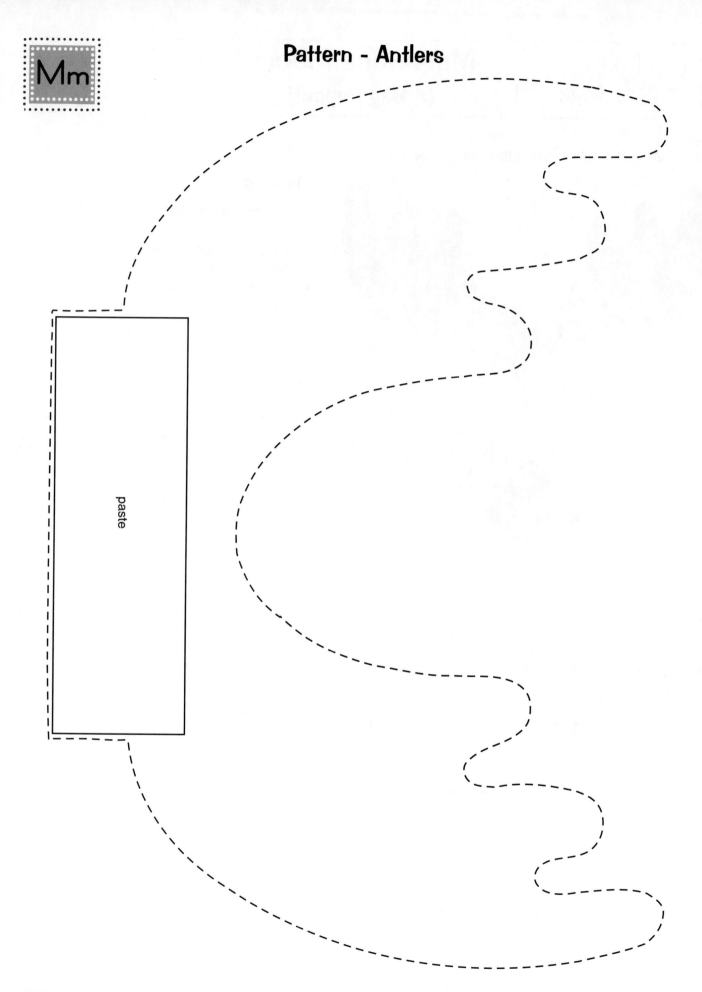

paste

Fun with the Alphabet EMC 774

Pattern - Head, Ears

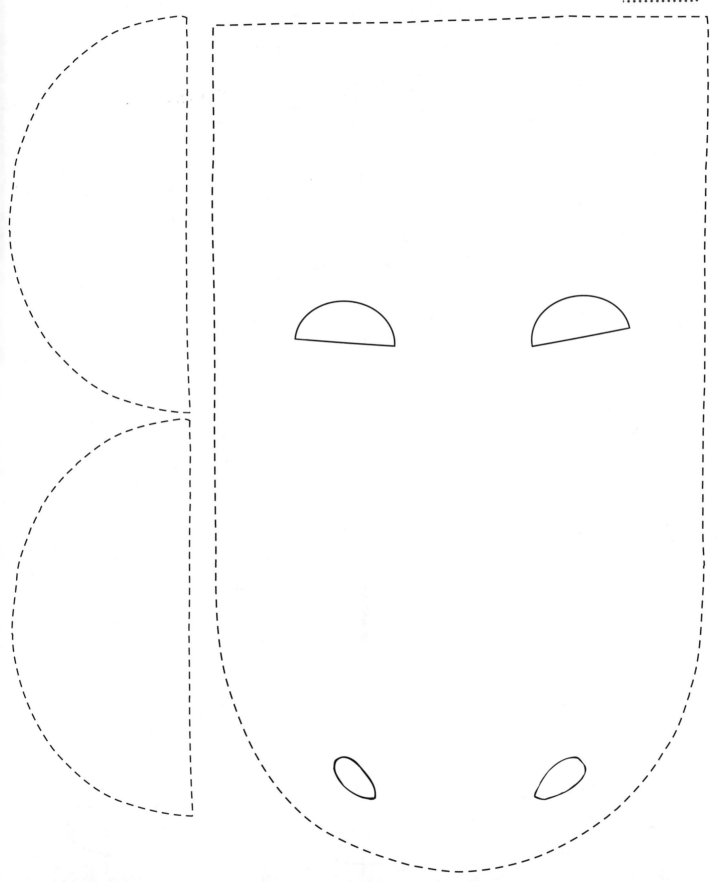

Mm

On the Moon

name

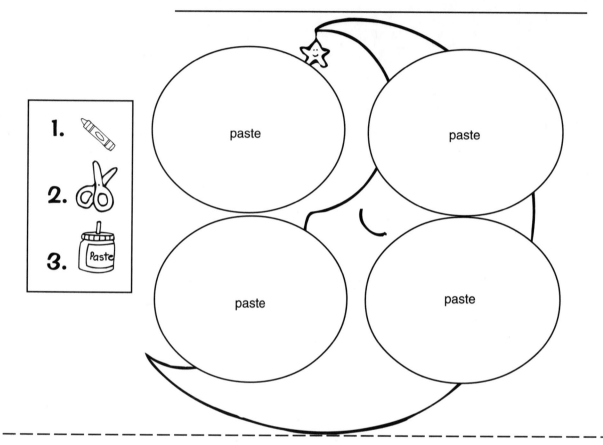

1.
2.
3. Paste

paste paste

paste paste

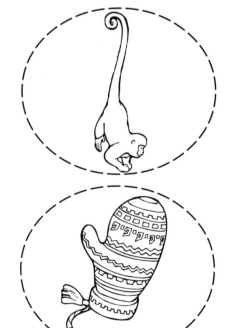

q

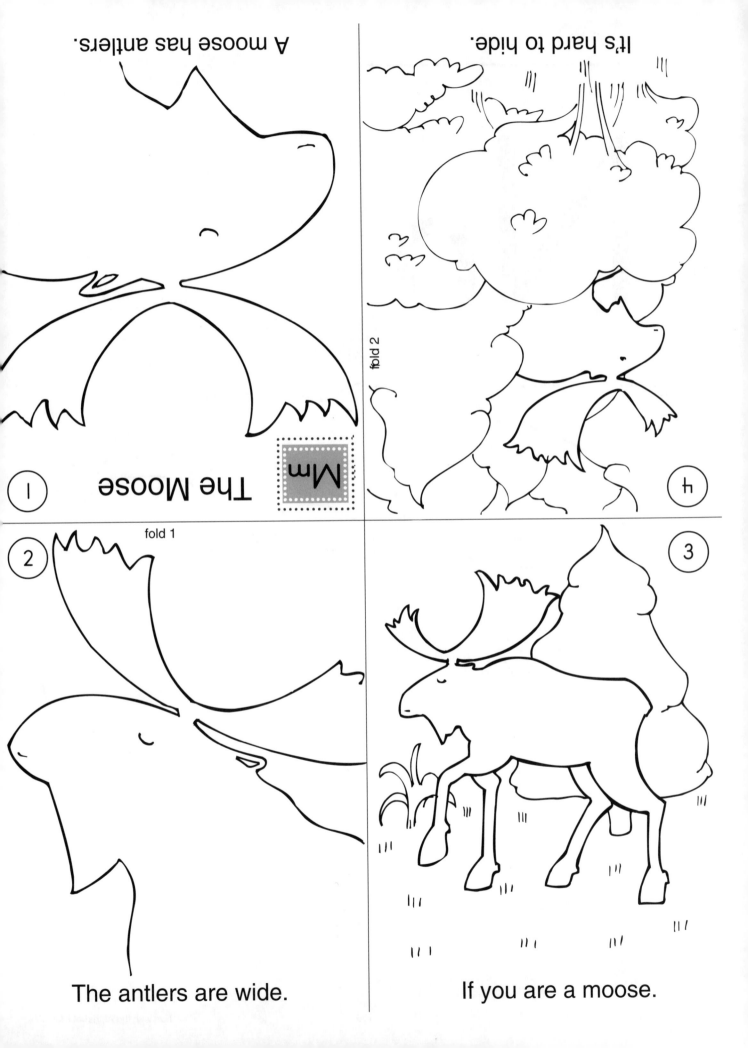

A moose has antlers.

The Moose

Mm

1

It's hard to hide.

fold 2

4

fold 1

2

The antlers are wide.

3

If you are a moose.

Pages four and five provide teaching ideas for introducing and practicing each letter. Use these in conjunction with the specific resources for "N" listed below.

Have students sort objects. Sort things starting with the sound "n" makes.

Alphabet Books:

A, B, See! by Tana Hoban; Greenwillow Books, 1982.

The Glorious ABC by Cooper Edens; Atheneum, 1990.

I Can Sign My ABCs by Susan Gibbon Chaplin; Gallaudet, 1986.

Books About Noodles and Necklaces:

A Taste of Italy by Jenny Ridgwell; Thomson Learning, 1993. (This book contains a chapter of information, illustrations, and recipes about pasta (pages 16 - 19). Share appropriate pages with your students.)

Put your favorite recipe using noodles on a chart and read it with your students as you would a poem or chant. Then consider cooking noodles and cheese for a class snack!

Books About Nests:

Are You My Mother? by P. D. Eastman; Random Books for Young Readers, 1960.

Flap Your Wings by P. D. Eastman; Random House Early Bird Book, 1969.

Stellaluna by Janell Cannon; Harcourt Brace Jovanovich, 1993.

Urban Roots: Where Birds Nest in the City by Barbara Bash; Little, Brown, 1990.

- 1 package Wheat Chex® and Rice Chex®
- 1 package of Cheerios®
- 1 package thin pretzel sticks
- 1 lb. (452 gm) salted nuts
- 1/4 lb. (113 gm) margarine
- 1/2 lb. (227 gm) melted butter
- 1 tsp. (5 ml) worchestershire sauce
- 1/2 tsp. (2 gm) garlic salt

1. Mix all ingredients in roasting pan.
2. Bake 200º F (93º C) for 2 hours. Stir occasionally.

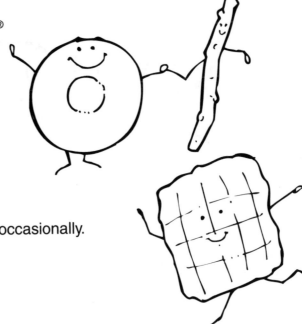

 Draw It!   **The Nest**

Direct students to fold a blank piece of paper into four sections. Draw on the chalkboard and use oral instructions to guide students to draw the following:

1. Make a brown nest.

2. Make a white egg in a brown nest.

3. Make a crack in an egg in a brown nest.

4. Make a surprise in a brown nest.

Oral Language Experience:

Students dictate a sentence or short story about one of the pictures to an adult.

 **Write It!**

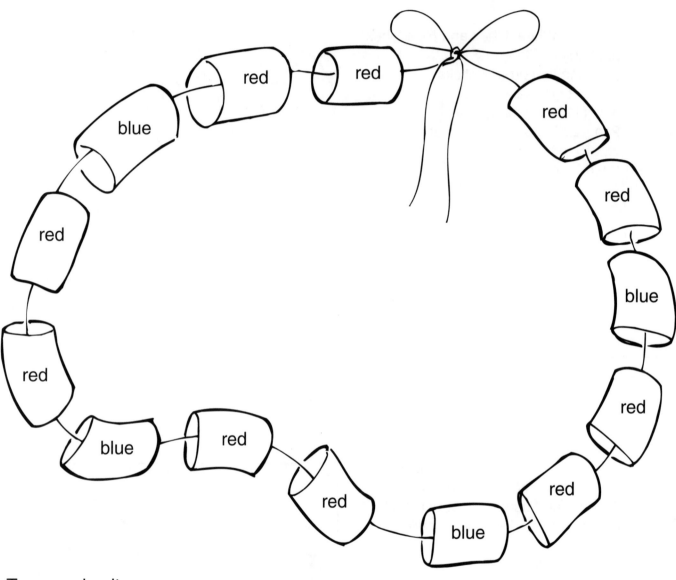

red

red

blue

red

red

red

red

blue

red

blue

red

red

red

blue

red

Trace and write.

n n n n n n

N N N N N

necklace

Make It! **Nifty Noodle Necklace**

It's always fun to wear jewelry you've made all by yourself!

Materials:

- Various sizes and styles of noodles. (Choose those that can be easily strung.)
- rubbing alcohol
- food coloring (3 bright colors)
- quart jar with well-fitting lid
- waxed paper
- 1 yard (91.5 cm) of heavy string
- masking tape
- tagboard for medallion (see patterns on page 142)
- white glue and glitter (for lettering the medallions)
- hole punch

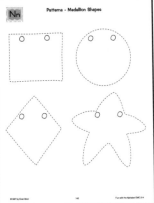

Teacher steps to follow:

1. Dye the noodles.

   a. Put 1/2" (1.25 cm) rubbing alcohol and 20 or more drops of food coloring in a quart jar. (Experiment to find the shade you like best.)

   b. Fill 2/3 full of noodles. Shake well. Spread the noodles on waxed paper to dry.

   c. Repeat for the two other colors.

2. Cut medallions from tag using the patterns on page 142. Punch 2 holes in each medallion.

3. Call up each child to select one medallion shape. Write the child's initials on the medallion with white glue. The child can sprinkle on glitter. Let it dry thoroughly!

Child's steps:

1. Tie one end of the string to the medallion.

2. Wrap masking tape around the other end of the string to make a "needle."

3. String the noodles. (You can use this as a time to practice patterning. Put a pattern on a strip of tag and place it in front of the child as a reference while stringing.)

4. When the necklace is the desired length, tie the open end to the other hole in the medallion. Cut off the excess string. Now it is ready to wear!

       Fun with the Alphabet EMC 774

Patterns - Medallion Shapes

Find the Pictures Hiding Here

Can you find these pictures that start with "n"?

Fun with the Alphabet EMC 774

Nn

In the Nest

name _____

- -

_____

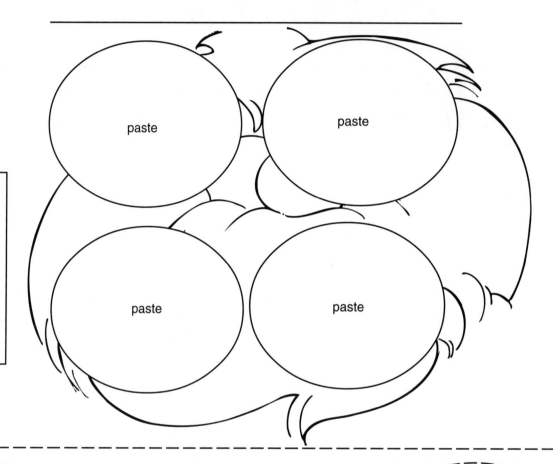

1. ✏️
2. ✂️
3. Paste

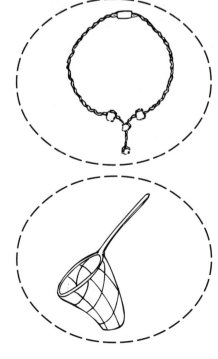

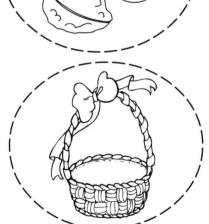

144

Fun with the Alphabet EMC 774

I made a necklace.

I made it out of noodles.

fold 2

Noodles

Nn

1

4

2

fold 1

I made a necklace.

I put the noodles on a string.

3

It took oodles and oodles.

146

Pages four and five provide teaching ideas for introducing and practicing each letter. Use these in conjunction with the specific resources for "A" listed below.

Have students sort objects. Sort things starting with the sound "o" makes.

Note: Determine whether you will introduce both the short and long sounds of the vowel at the same time.

Alphabet Books:

Alligator Arrived with Apples: A Potluck Alphabet Feast by Crescent Dragonwagon; Macmillan, 1987.

On Market Street by Arnold Lobel; Greenwillow Books, 1981.

Potluck by Anne Shelby; Orchard Books, 1993.

Books About Otters:

Otter on His Own: The Story of a Sea Otter by Doe Boyle; Soundprints, 1995.

Otters (Cousteau Society); Little Simon, 1993.

Otters by Emilie U. Lepthien; Children's Press, 1994.

A Raft of Sea Otters by Vicki Leon; Silver Burdett, 1995. (Use appropriate pages.)

Sea Elf by Joanne Ryder; Morrow Junior Books, 1993.

Swim the Silver Sea by Nancy White Carlstron; Philomel Books, 1993.

Books About an Octopus:

An Octopus Is Amazing by Patricia Lauber; Crowell, 1996. (Use appropriate pages.)

Down in the Sea: The Octopus by Patricia Kite; Albert Whitman, 1993.

How to Hide An Octopus by Ruth Heller; Grosset & Dunlap, 1985. (Use appropriate pages.)

My Very Own Octopus by Bernard Most; Harcourt Brace Jovanovich, 1980.

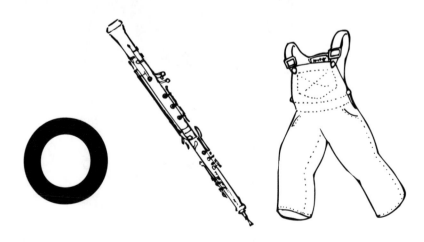

 **Eat It!** **Olive Tasting Time!**

Try black olives, green olives, and for brave little children...olives with pimento!

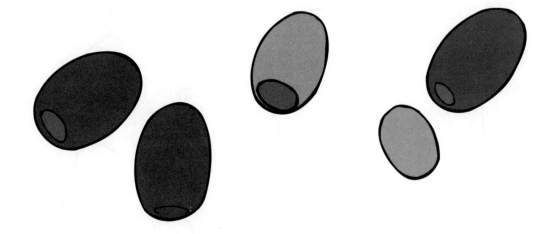

 Draw It! **An Octopus**

Direct students to fold a blank piece of paper into four sections. Draw on the chalkboard and use oral instructions to guide students to draw the following:

1. Make an octopus.

2. Make an octopus holding shells.

3. Make an octopus peeking out of a cave.

4. Make an octopus swimming through the water.

Oral Language Experience:

Students dictate a sentence or short story about one of the pictures to an adult.

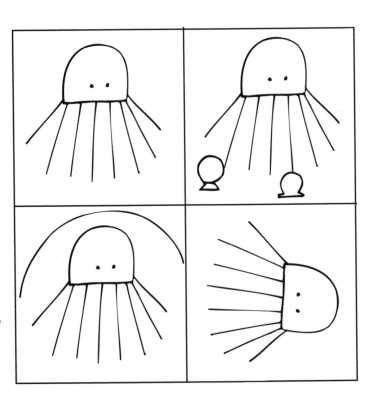

name

_____

Write It!

How many ◯ in the ⬭ ?

Trace and write.

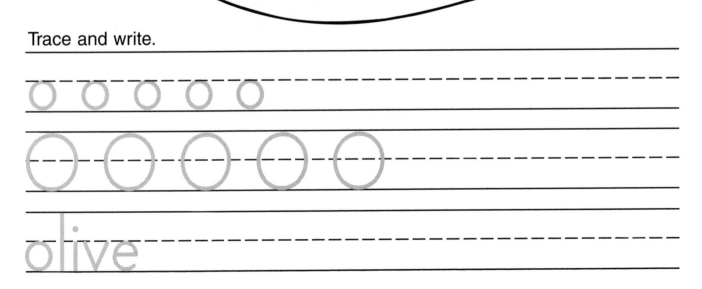

O O O O O

O O O O O

olive

This little sea otter is enjoying his lunch.

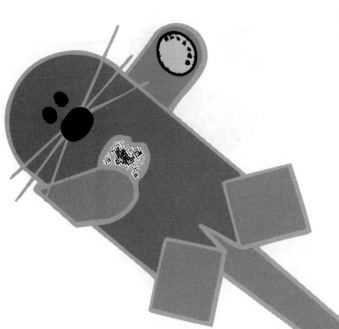

Materials:

- reproducible patterns on pages 152 and 153
- brown construction paper
- black construction paper:
  6 thin strips 3" (7.5 cm) long (for whiskers)
- crayons
- scissors
- paste
- cellophane tape

Optional:

Light brown, gray, or white construction paper for a shell and rock OR a real pebble and shell.

Steps to follow:

1. Cut out the pattern pieces.

2. Cut the slit up from the bottom of the body to form the hind legs. Fold the feet up.

3. Paste the front paws on the back of the body, leaving about 5" (13 cm) for the head. Paste the tail on the back of the body above the leg slit.

4. Put the whiskers on the otter's face. (Tape will help to hold the whiskers in place.)

Optional:

Cut a shell from gray, white, or light brown construction paper, or use a real pebble and a real shell. Paste the rock on the otter's chest.
Paste the shell on the otter's front paw. Bend the paw so the otter can "pound" the shell on the rock to break it open.

       Fun with the Alphabet EMC 774

Pattern - Body, Arms, Tail

Who Is This?

Fun with the Alphabet EMC 774

Fill the Oval

name

paste paste

paste paste

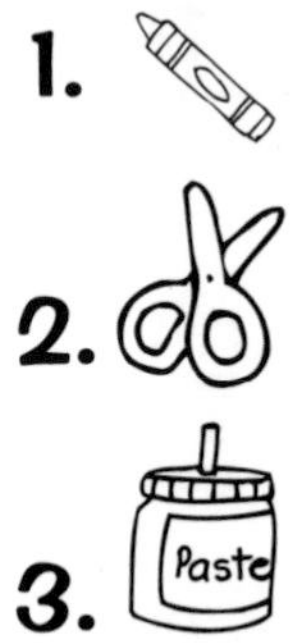

1.
2.
3. Paste

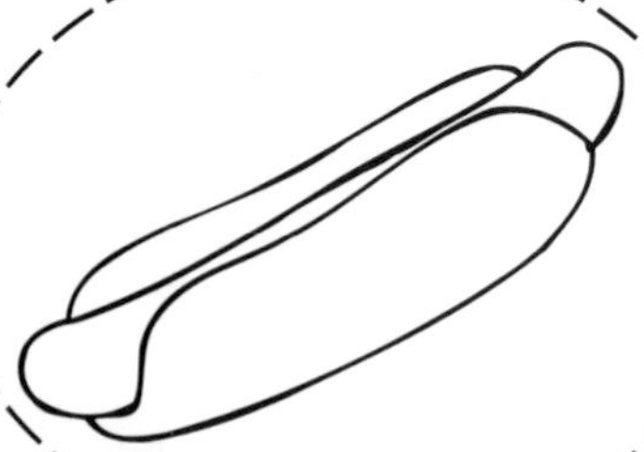

The otter floats on its back.

The Otter

1

What a tasty lunch.

fold 2

4

fold 1

2

It's cracking abalone.

3

Can you hear the crunch?

156

Pages four and five provide teaching ideas for introducing and practicing each letter. Use these in conjunction with the specific resources for "P" listed below.

Have students sort objects. Put things starting with the sound "p" makes in a purse.

Alphabet Books:

Pedro, His Perro, and the Alphabet Sombrero by Lynn Rowe Reed; Hyperion Books for Children, 1995.

Pigs Alphabet by Leah P. Preiss; Grodine, 1989.

Pigs from A to Z by Arthur Geisert; Houghton Mifflin, 1986.

Books About Pigs:

Emmett's Pig (An I Can Read Book) by Mary Stolz; Harper, 1959.

The Fourth Little Pig by Teresa Noel Celsi; Raintree Steck Vaughn, 1990.

Geraldine First by Holly Keller; Greenwillow Books, 1996.

Little Pink Pig by Pat Hutchins; Greenwillow Books, 1994.

Oliver and Amanda and the Big Snow by Jean Van Leeuwen; Dial Books for Young Readers, 1995.

Picnic with Piggins by Jane Yolen; Harcourt Brace Jovanovich, 1988.

Piggy in the Puddle by Charlotte Pomerantz; Simon & Schuster, 1989.

Pigs by Robert Munsch; Firefly Books, 1989.

Pigs Aplenty, Pigs Galore! by David Mcphail; Dutton Children's Books, 1993.

Pigs (Farm Animals Discovery Library) by Lynn Stone; Rourke, 1990.

Small Pig by Arnold Lobel; Harper & Row, 1969.

Tom's Tail by Linda Jennings; Little, Brown, 1995.

Yummers Too: The Second Course by James Marshall; Houghton Mifflin, 1986.

Books About Popcorn:

The Popcorn Book by Tomie De Paola; Holiday House, 1978.

Popcorn Dragon by Jane Thayer; Morrow Junior Books, 1989.

Popcorn Shop (Hello Reader Series) by Alice Low; Scholastic, 1994.

Taste all types of pickles. Be sure to include watermelon pickles and pickled pigs' feet!

If your group isn't too adventurous, have a popcorn party instead.

 Draw It!   **Popcorn**

Direct students to fold a blank piece of paper into four sections. Draw on the chalkboard and use oral instructions to guide students to draw the following:

1. Make a piece of popcorn popping out of a pan.

2. Make two pieces of popcorn popping out of a pan.

3. Make lots of popcorn popping out of a pan.

4. Make a popcorn ball out of all the popcorn.

Oral Language Experience:

Students dictate a sentence or short story about one of the pictures to an adult.

P p

name

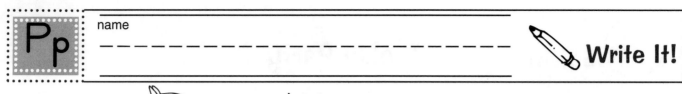

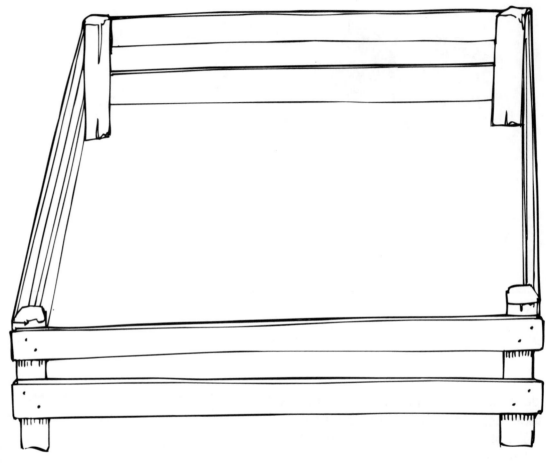

Make three in the .

Trace and write.

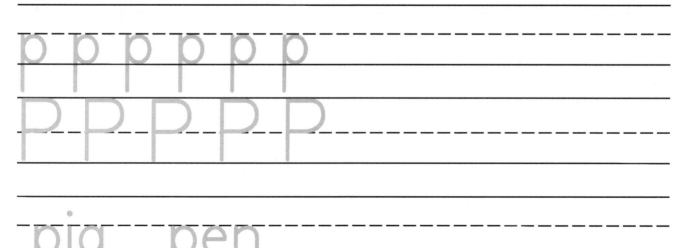

p p p p p

P P P P P

pig   pen

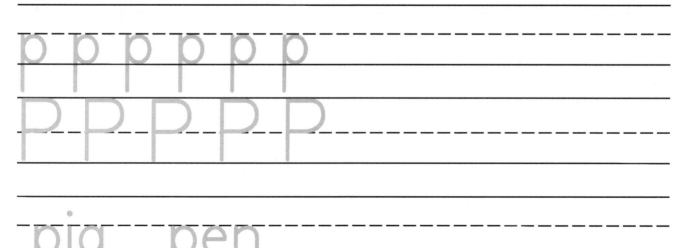

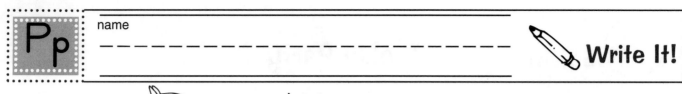

 **Make It!** # Perky Pink Pig

This charming pig is fun to make. It can be easily turned into a puppet. Simply paste it onto a tongue depressor. Now you are all set to act out your favorite pig poem or story.

Materials:

- reproducible pattern pieces on page 162
- pink construction paper
- 1- 1 1/2" x 3" (4 x 7.5 cm) strip pink construction paper
- black crayon
- scissors
- paste

Optional:

- tongue depressor

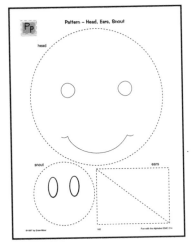

Steps to follow:

1. Cut out the pattern pieces.

2. Color the oval nostrils on the snout. (This is a good time to talk about the differences between an oval and a circle.)

3. Make the pink strip into a cylinder. Put paste on one end and roll the paper. Hold the cylinder closed and count to 10. This gives the paste time to set.

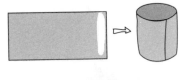

4. Paste the snout on one side of the cylinder. Paste the other side of the cylinder to the pig's face. This will make the snout stand out.

5. Paste the ears on the head.

6. Use a crayon to draw the eyes and a mouth. Children who finish early may want to add a flower behind one ear or a hat on top, so have scraps of construction paper handy.

Optional

- turn your pig into a puppet.

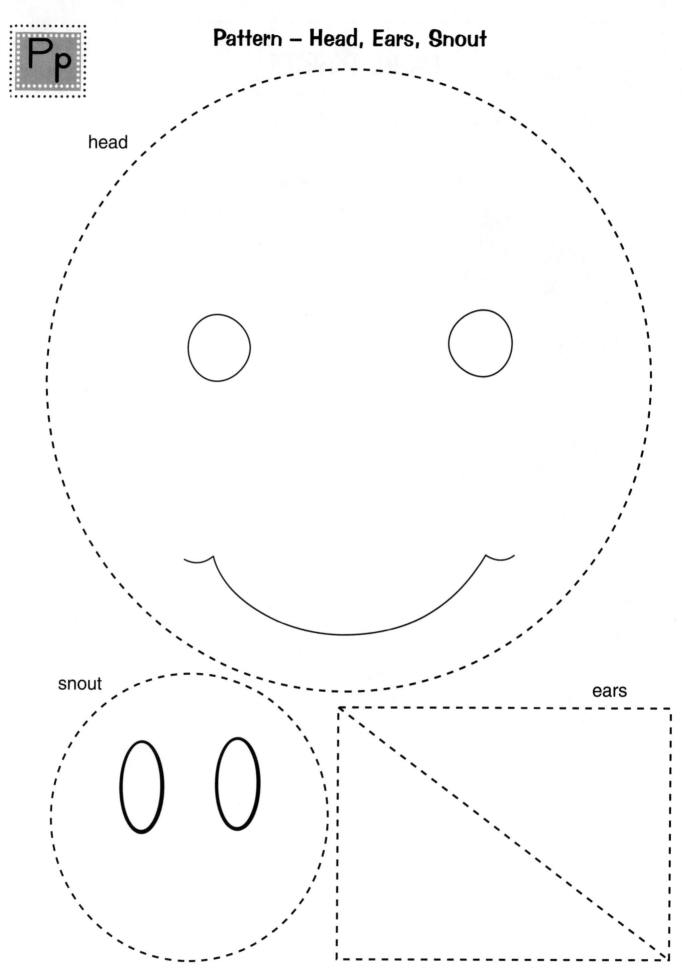

Pattern – Head, Ears, Snout

P p

head

snout

ears

Put the Puzzle Pieces Together

paste here

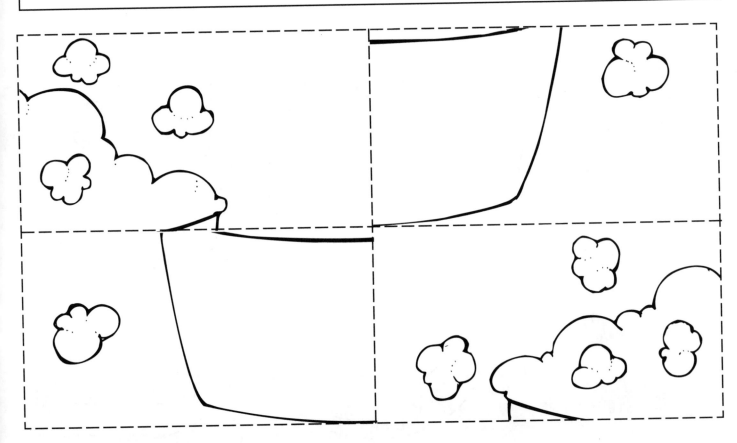

163

Fun with the Alphabet EMC 774

Fill the Pail

name _____

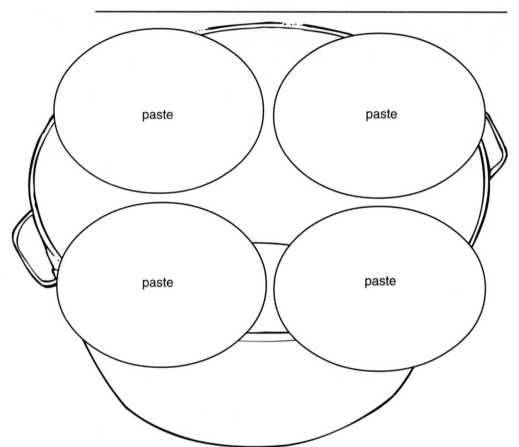

paste   paste

paste   paste

1.
2.
3. Paste

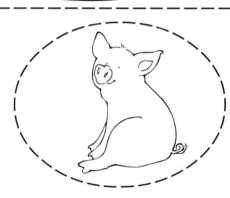

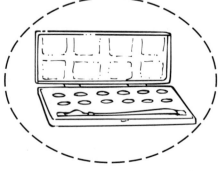

Pink Pig

① My Pig

Pp

fold 1

② Pretty Pink Pig

fold 2

Pretty Pink Pig poses for a picture.

④

③ Pretty Pink Pig poses.

166

 **Learn It!** # Teaching the Letter

Pages four and five provide teaching ideas for introducing and practicing each letter. Use these in conjunction with the specific resources for "Q" listed below.

Have students sort objects. Put things starting with the sound "q" makes in a quart container.

Fun with the Alphabet EMC 774

Bibliography

 **Read It!**

Alphabet Books:

Alphabet Times Four - An International ABC by Ruth Brown; Dutton, 1991.

Alphabet Soup by Kate Banks; Knopf, 1994.

Chicka Chicka Boom Boom by Bill Martin, Jr. & John Archambault; Simon & Schuster, 1989.

Books About Quail:

State Birds by Arthur Singer & Alan Singer; Lodestar Books/Dutton, 1986. (Share the pictures and information on pages 16 and 17 with your students.)

Read the "q" verse from ***The ABC Bunny*** by Wanda Gag; Putnam, 1978.

Read the "q" page from any of Edward Lear's nonsense alphabets. (One source is ***Nonsense Books*** by Edward Lear; Little, Brown). You will also find them in many poetry anthologies.

Books About Quilts :

Ernest and Celestine's Patchwork Quilt by Gabrielle Vincent; Greenwillow Books, 1982.

Josefina y la colcha de retazos (***Josefina Story Quilt*** in Spanish) translated by Aida Marcuse; Harper Arco Iris, 1995.

Josephina Story Quilt by Eleanor Coerr; Harper Trophy, 1986.

The Keeping Quilt by Patricia Polacco; Simon & Schuster, 1988.

Luka's Quilt by Georgia Guback; Greenwillow Books, 1994.

Sweet Clara and the Freedom Quilt by Deborah Hopkinson; Knopf, 1993.

Quilt by Ann Jonas; Greenwillow Books, 1984.

 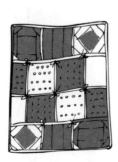 

Fun with the Alphabet EMC 774

Quite Tasty Quilt

Create edible "quilt squares" with soda crackers or graham crackers.

- Use these on soda crackers:
  cream cheese
  peanut butter
  "squeeze" cheese

  Add color with bits of vegetables, nuts, candied fruits, or chocolate bits.

- Use frosting on graham crackers.

 Draw It!   **Quilts**

Direct students to fold a blank piece of paper into four sections. Draw on the chalkboard and use oral instructions to guide students to draw the following:

1. Make a quilt with red ends and a red circle.

2. Make a quilt. Divide it into quarters. Put a blue square in each quarter.

3. Make a quilt with lace around the edge.

4. Make a surprise quilt for a queen. Make it colorful.

Oral Language Experience:

Students dictate a sentence or short story about one of the pictures to an adult.

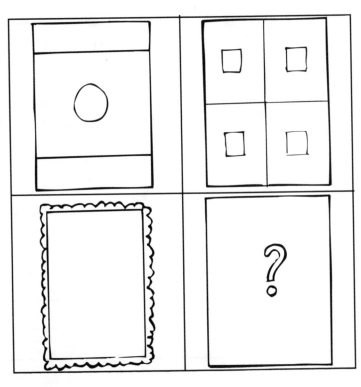

name

_ _

 **Write It!**

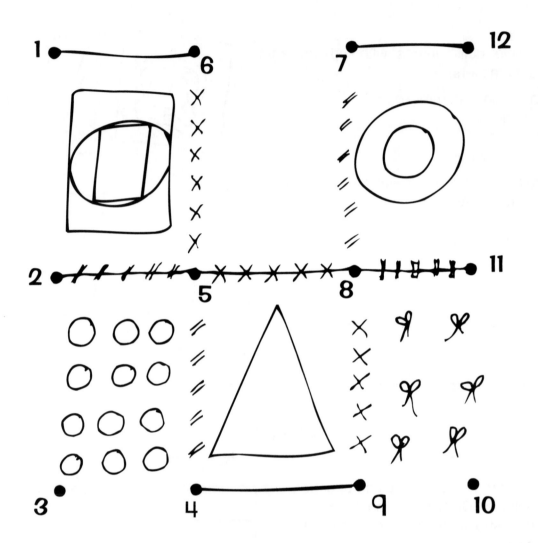

Trace and write.

q q q q q

Q Q Q Q

quilt

 **Make It!**

Quiet Quail

Father Quail leads a covey of babies out on their morning search for food.

Materials:

- Reproduce the quail family pattern on page 172 on white construction paper.
- green construction paper 6" x 18" (15 cm x 45.5 cm)
- scissors
- crayons
- paste

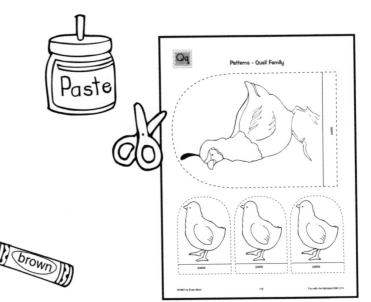

Steps to follow:

1. Color the quail brown.

2. Cut on the dotted lines.

3. Fold the flaps under and paste the quail to the green paper.

 Fun with the Alphabet EMC 774

Patterns - Quail Family

paste

paste

paste

paste

Find a baby quail hiding in this picture.

Fun with the Alphabet EMC 774

Qq

On the Quilt

name

1.

2.

3.

paste

paste

paste

paste

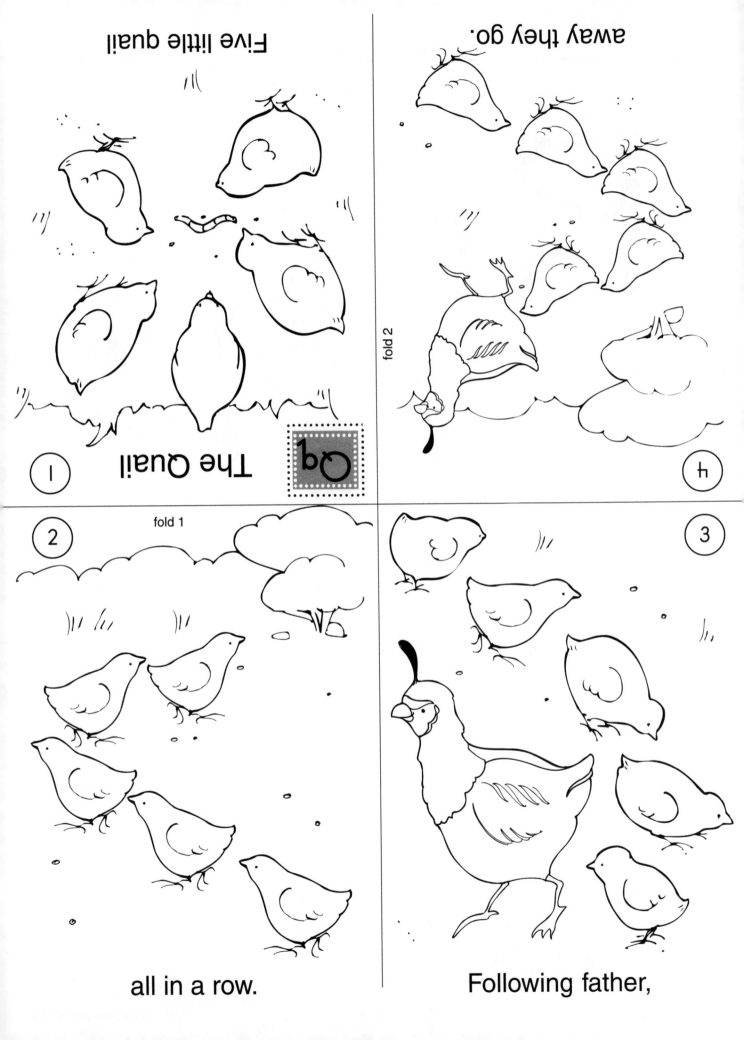

Five little quail

The Quail

Qq

1

away they go.

fold 2

4

fold 1

2

all in a row.

3

Following father,

Rr

Pages four and five provide teaching ideas for introducing and practicing each letter. Use these in conjunction with the specific resources for "R" listed below.

Have students sort objects. Look for things starting with the sound "r" makes.

Alphabet Books:

A Is For Astronaut by Sian Tucker; Little Simon, 1995.

A Was An Angler by Janina Domanska; Greenwillow Books, 1985.

Eating the Alphabet A to Z by Lois Ehlert; Harcourt Brace Jovanovich, 1989

Richard Scarry's Find Your ABC's; Random House Pictureback, 1973.

Books About Raccoons:

The Case of the Two Masked Robbers by Lillian Hoban; Harper & Row, 1986.

Little Raccoon Who Could by Susan C. Poskanzer; Troll Communications, 1986.

Raccoons by Lynn Stone; Rourke, 1990. (Use appropriate pages.)

Raccoons & Ripe Corn by Jim Arnosky; Morrow, 1995.

Raccoon Connections by Grace E. Lassik; Four Star Publications, 1992.

Raccon's Tale by Graham Percy; Random House Books for Young Readers, 1995.

Books About Robots:

Get Ready for Robots! by Patricia Lauber; Crowell, 1987.

Robots: Here They Come! (Discovery World Series) by Janet Riehecky; Child's World, 1990.

Robots - What They Are, What They Do by Fredericka Berger; Greenwillow Books, 1992.

- 2 cups (176 gm) uncooked instant rice
- 3 cups (711 ml) milk
- 6 tbs. (72 gm) sugar
- 1/2 tsp. (2 gm) salt
- 1/2 tsp. (2 gm) cinnamon
- 1/2 cup (57 gm) seedless raisins

1. Combine all ingredients in a sauce pan.

2. Bring to a full rolling boil. Stir constantly.

3. Remove from heat and let stand 12-15 minutes, stirring occasionally. Serve warm or cool.

 Draw It!   **The Robot**

Direct students to fold a blank piece of paper into four sections. Draw on the chalkboard and use oral instructions to guide students to draw the following:

1. Make Rocky Robot. Color him red.

2. Make Roberta Robot. She is blue.

3. Make Ringo Robot orange.

4. Make poor Ray Robot. He stayed out in the rain. He is all rusty now.

Oral Language Experience:

Students dictate a sentence or short story about one of the pictures to an adult.

Rr

 **Write It!**

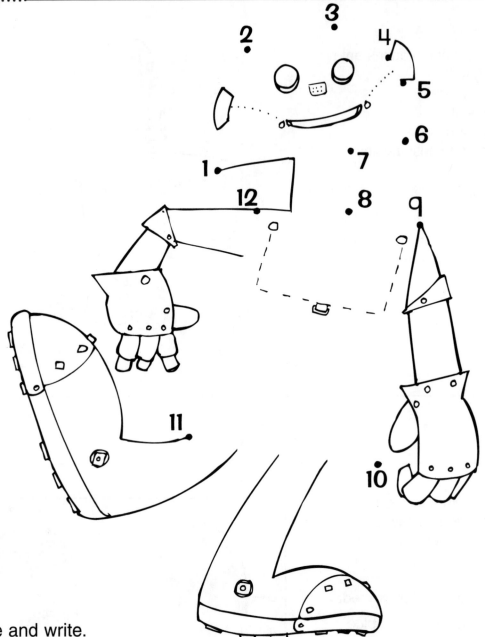

Trace and write.

r r r r r

R R R R

robot

Raccoon Mask

Children will love telling facts and stories about raccoons while wearing these delightful makes. (Cut out eye holes before giving the mask to students.)

Materials:

- reproducible mask pattern (page 182)
- white paper
- crayons
- hole punch
- 2- 12" (30.5 cm) pieces of yarn

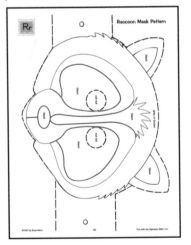

Steps to follow:

1. Color the mask. Leave unlabeled areas white as shown above.

2. Cut on the dotted lines.

3. Punch holes through the circles on the mask flaps.

4. Tie the yarn pieces through the holes.

Fun with the Alphabet EMC 774

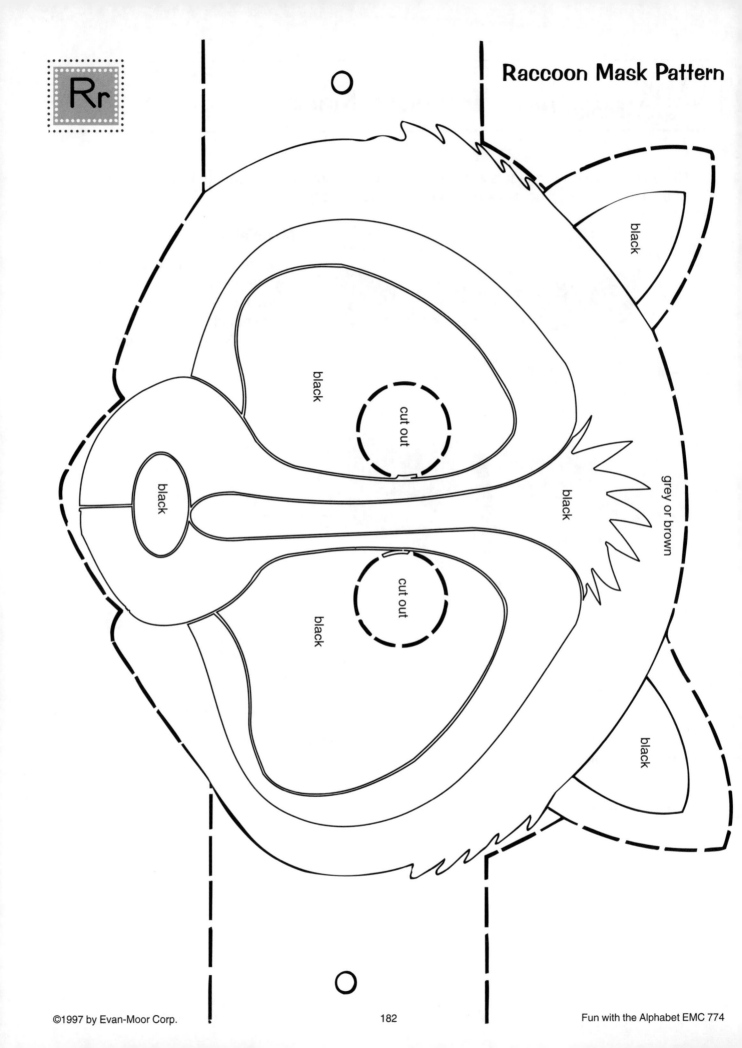

Raccoon Mask Pattern

black

black

cut out

black

black

cut out

black

grey or brown

black

182

Fun with the Alphabet EMC 774

Robot Puzzle

Fun with the Alphabet EMC 774

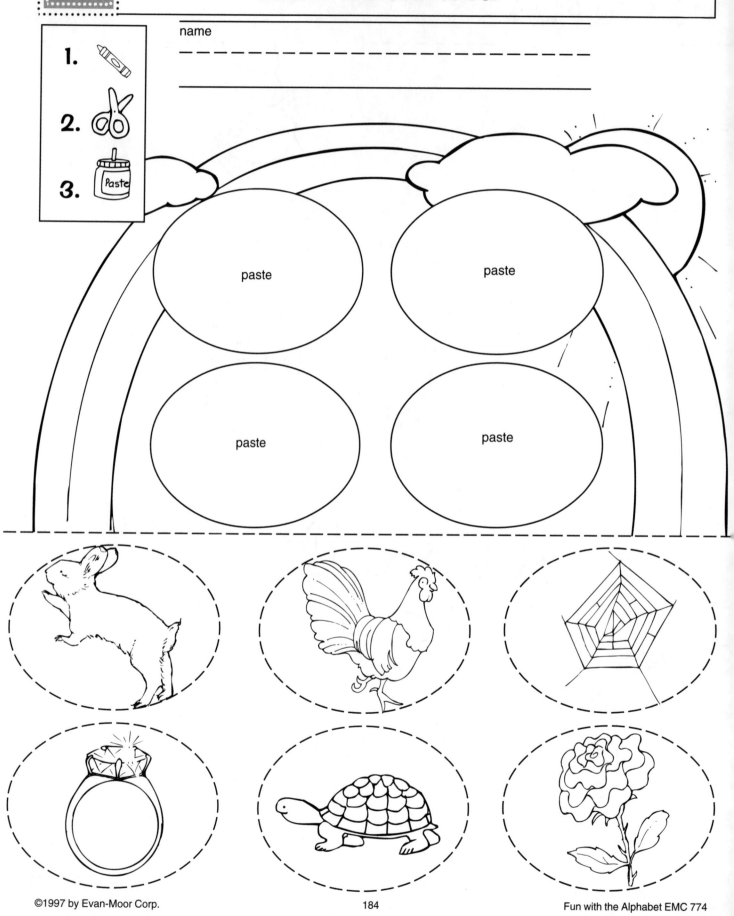

Rr

Under the Rainbow

name

1. *(crayon)*
2. *(scissors)*
3. *(Paste)*

paste

paste

paste

paste

184

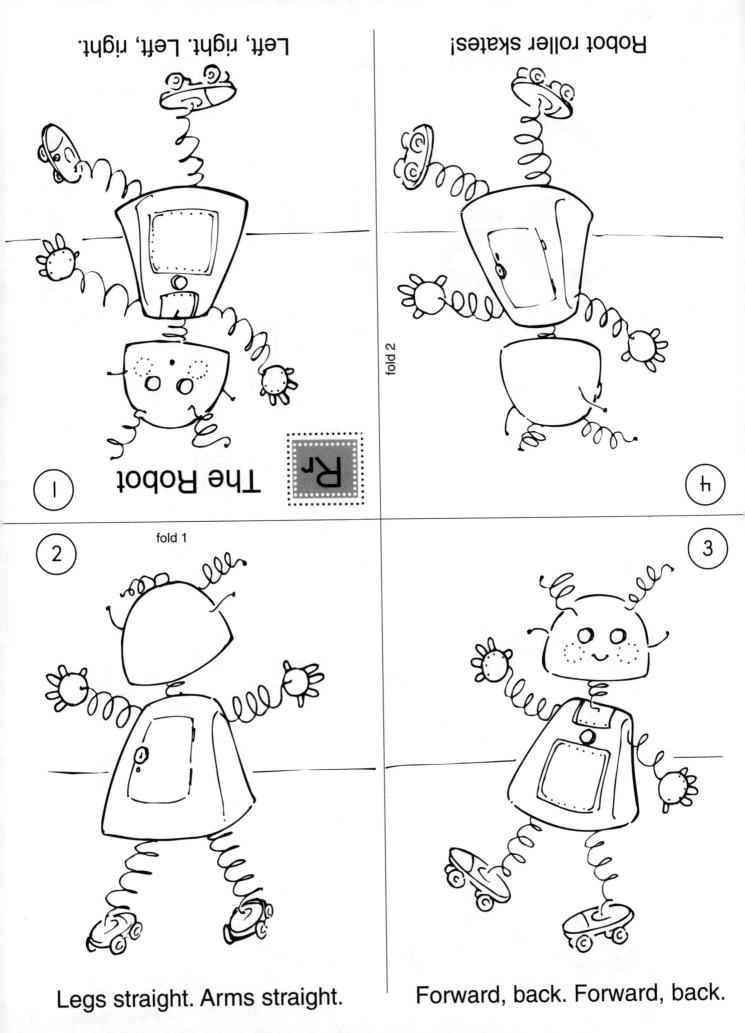

Left, right. Left, right.

Robot roller skates!

The Robot

Rr

① fold 1

② Legs straight. Arms straight.

③ Forward, back. Forward, back.

④ fold 2

S s

186

Fun with the Alphabet EMC 774

Pages four and five provide teaching ideas for introducing and practicing each letter. Use these in conjunction with the specific resources for "S" listed below.

Have students sort objects. Put things starting with the sound "s" makes in a suitcase.

Alphabet Books:

In a Pumpkin Shell: A Mother Goose ABC by Joan Walsh Anglund; Harcourt Brace, 1960.

Demi's Find the Animals ABC by Demi; Putnam, 1989.

Zoo Alphabet Book by Diane Hill; Hill Associates, 1995.

Books About Skunks:

Skunk at Hemlock Circle by Victoria Sherrow; Soundprints, 1994.

Skunks (New True Book) by Emilie U. Lepthien; Children's Press, 1993.

Skunks by Lynn Stone; Rourke, 1990. (Use appropriate pages.)

Books About Spiders:

Eentsy, Weentsy Spider: Fingerplays & Action Rhymes by Joanna Cole & Stephanie Calmenson; Morrow Junior Books, 1991.

The Lady and the Spider by Faith McNulty; Harper & Row, 1986.

Spider by David Howcock; Random House Books for Young Readers, 1994

Spiders by Gail Gibbons; Holiday House, 1994.

Spider's Lunch: All About Garden Spiders (All Aboard Reading Series) by Joanna Cole; Grosset & Dunlap, 1995.

Spider Watching (Read & Wonder Series) by Vivian French; Candlewick Press, 1995.

Spider's Web (Stopwatch Series) by Christine Beck & Barrie Watts; Silver Press, 1986.

Very Busy Spider by Eric Carle; Philomel Books, 1985.

 **Eat It!**   # Sticky Spaghetti

1. Cook the spaghetti in a small pan with less water than usual. Overcook the spaghetti.

2. Drain the spaghetti, but don't rinse it. Cool the spaghetti. (This much can be done at home if you prefer. Store in a plastic bag in the refrigerator until ready to use.)

3. Each child gets a portion to nibble on as he or she creates a picture on construction paper using one or two strands. They will not need glue. This is really sticky spaghetti!

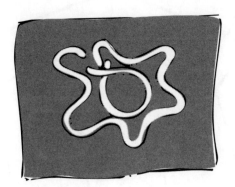

 Draw It!   # The Spider

Direct students to fold a blank piece of paper into four sections. Draw on the chalkboard and use oral instructions to guide students to draw the following:

1. Make a brown spider. He must have 8 legs.

2. Make a red spider on a green leaf.

3. Make a black spider hanging from his thread.

4. Make a green spider walking up a wall.

Oral Language Experience:

Students dictate a sentence or short story about one of the pictures to an adult.

Ss

name

Write It!

Make a 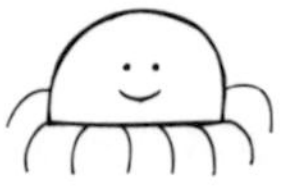 on the 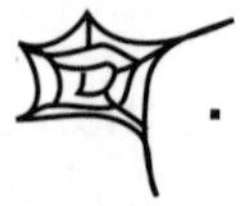 .

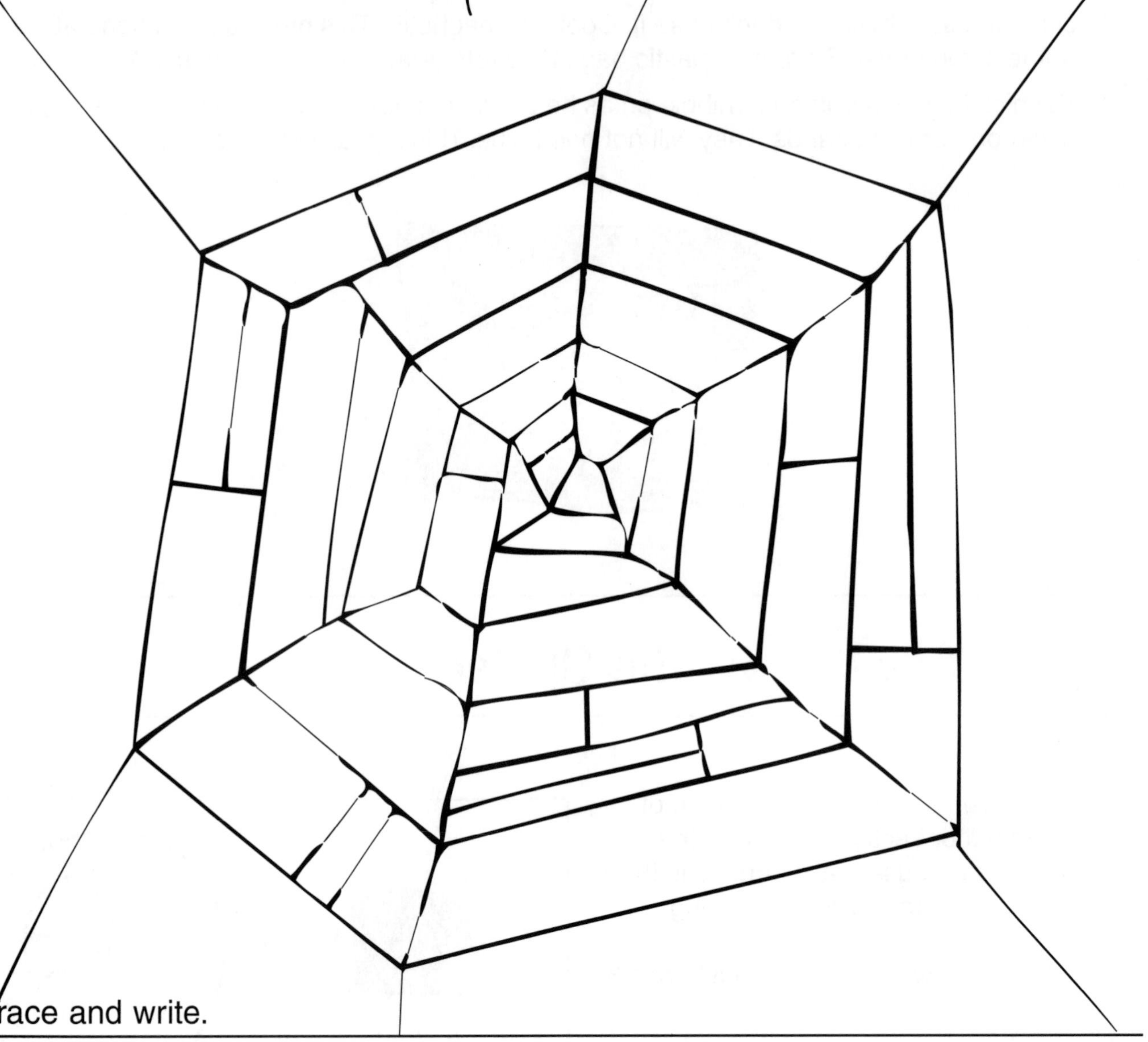

Trace and write.

s s s s s s

S S S S S

spider

Sweet Skunk

These are the kind of "little stinkers" you like to have around your classroom.

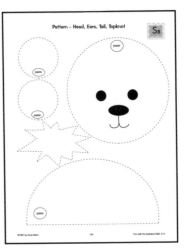

Materials:

- reproducible patterns on pages 192 and 193
- 2 – 1 1/2" x 10" (4 x 25.5cm) white construction paper
- paper fastener
- scissors
- paste
- black crayons

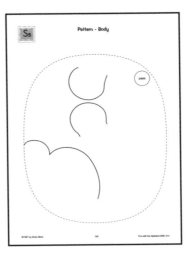

Steps to follow:

1. Color the body, head, and ears black. Leave the topknot white.
2. Cut out the pattern pieces.
3. Paste a white stripe to the body and a white strip to the tail. Trim off the excess.
4. Paste the head, and body together. The head will cover part of the stripe on the body.
5. Paste the ears on the back of the head. Paste the topknot to the head between the ears.
6. Attach the tail to the body of the skunk with the paper fastener. (The tail can be moved up and down.)

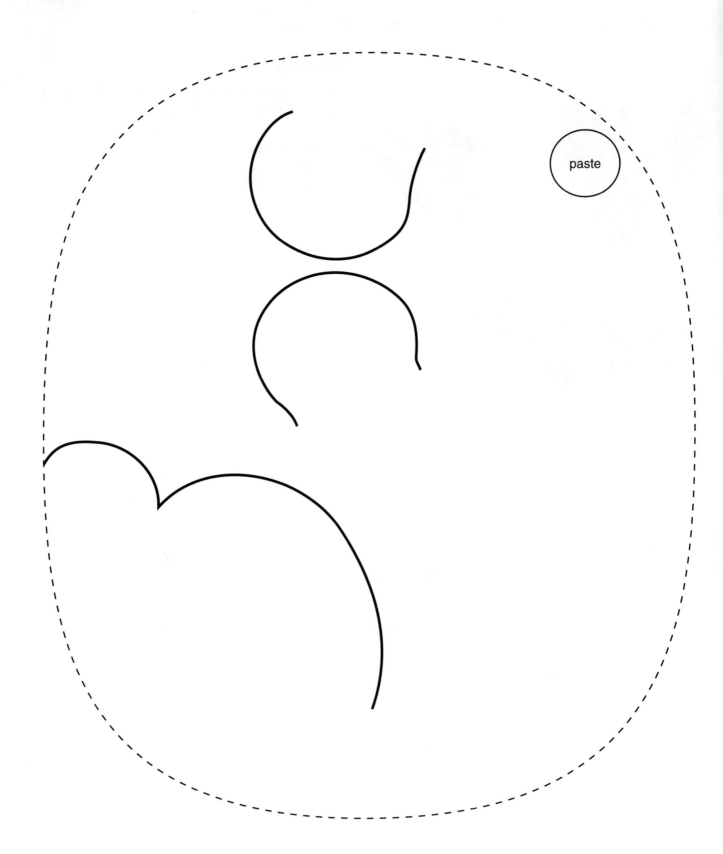

Pattern - Head, Ears, Tail, Topknot

Fun with the Alphabet EMC 774

Fill the Sack

name

1.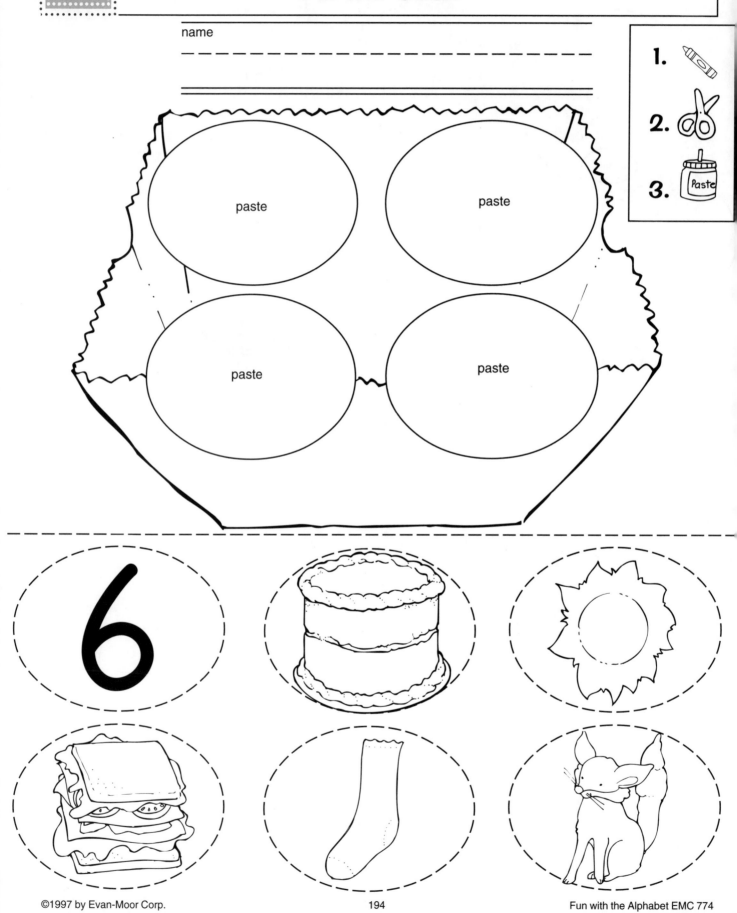
2.
3. Paste

paste

paste

paste

paste

6

Fun with the Alphabet EMC 774

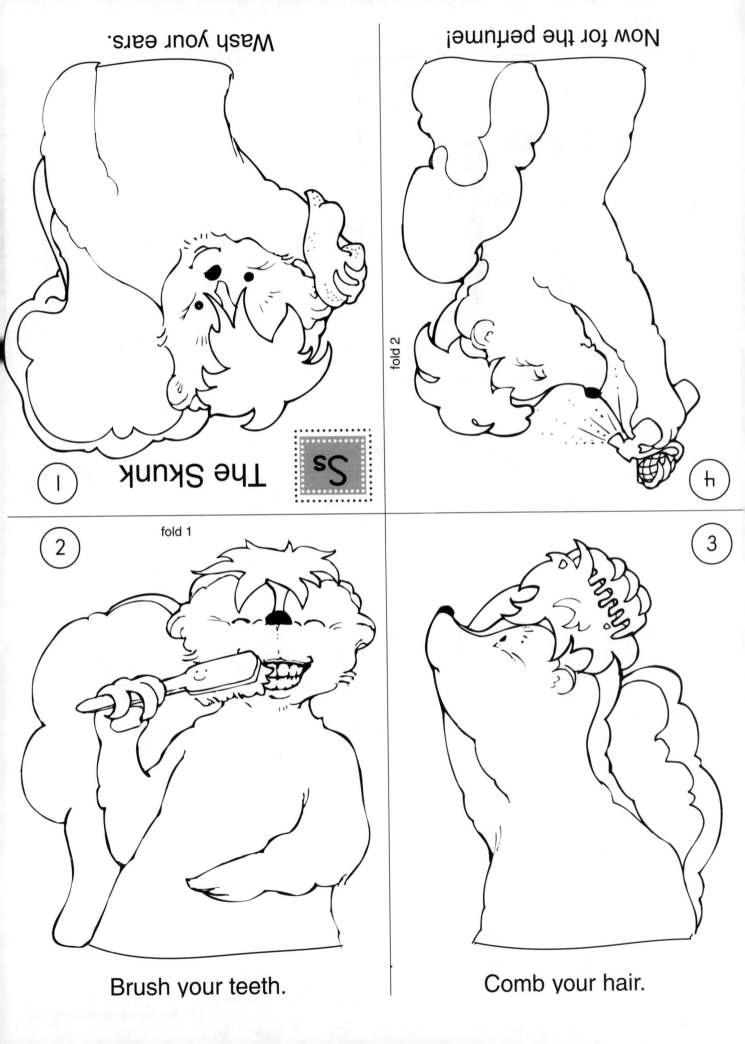

Wash your ears.

Now for the perfume!

The Skunk

Ss

1

fold 2

4

2

fold 1

3

Brush your teeth.

Comb your hair.

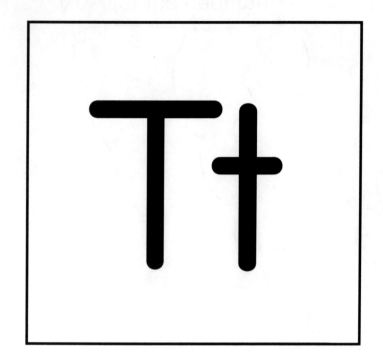

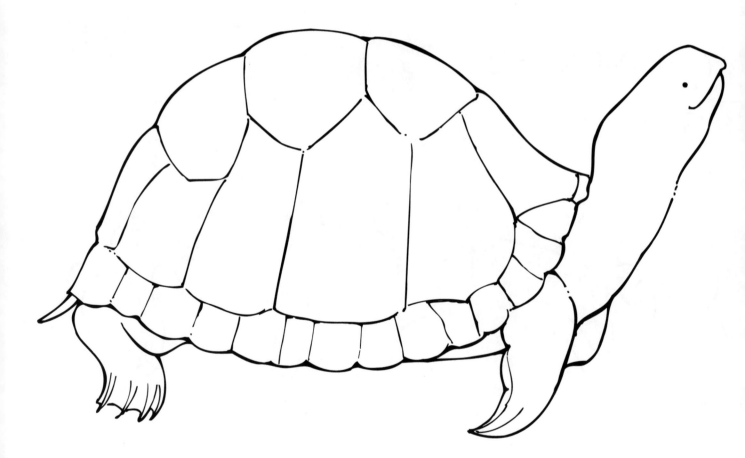

 **Learn It!**

Teaching the Letter

 Tt

Pages four and five provide teaching ideas for introducing and practicing each letter. Use these in conjunction with the specific resources for "T" listed below.

Have students sort objects. Put things starting with the sound "t" makes in a tote bag.

Bibliography

 **Read It!**

Alphabet Books:

Abracadabra to Zigzag by Nancy Lehman; Puffin, 1991.

A Helpful Alphabet of Friendly Objects by John Updike; Knopf, 1995.

City Seen from A to Z by Rachel Isadora; Greenwillow Books, 1983.

Books About Telephones:

A First Book of Do's and Don'ts by Ellen Weise; Random House Books for Young Readers, 1986.

Telephones, Televisions, and Toilets: How They Work and What Can Go Wrong by Melvin & Gilda Berger; Hambleton-Hill, 1993.

What Was It Like Before the Telephone? by Paul Humphrey; Steck-Vaughn, 1995.

Read the poem "Eletelphony" by Laura E. Richards. You will find it in many poetry anthologies. For example, ***Sing a Song of Popcorn: Every Child's Book of Poems*** selected by Beatrice Schenk de Regnier; Scholastic, 1988.

Books About Toast and Toasters:

Dog For a Day by Dick Gackenbach; Clarion, 1987.

The Little Pigs' First Cookbook by N. Cameron Watson; Little, Brown, 1987. (Share the recipe for Toast Francais (page 17) with your students.

Sounds All Around by Jane Belk Moncure; Children's Press, 1982.

Read the poem "The Toaster" by William Jay Smith. You will find it in many poetry anthologies. For example, ***Stuff and Nonsense*** compiled by Laura Cecil; Greenwillow Books, 1989.

Eat It! **Toast and Tasty Toppings**

Toast your favorite kind of bread.

Add some tasty toppings:
• Butter and jam
• Peanut butter and banana rounds
• Cream cheese and sweet pickles

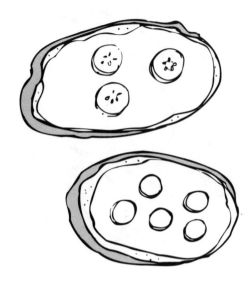

 Draw It! **Toast**

Direct students to fold a blank piece of paper into four sections. Draw on the chalkboard and use oral instructions to guide students to draw the following:

1. Make toast with butter.

2. Make toast with cheese.

3. Make toast with jam. A bite is missing.

4. Make burnt toast.

Oral Language Experience:

Students dictate a sentence or short story about one of the pictures to an adult.

12 11 10

1

2

9

3

8

7

4

5 6

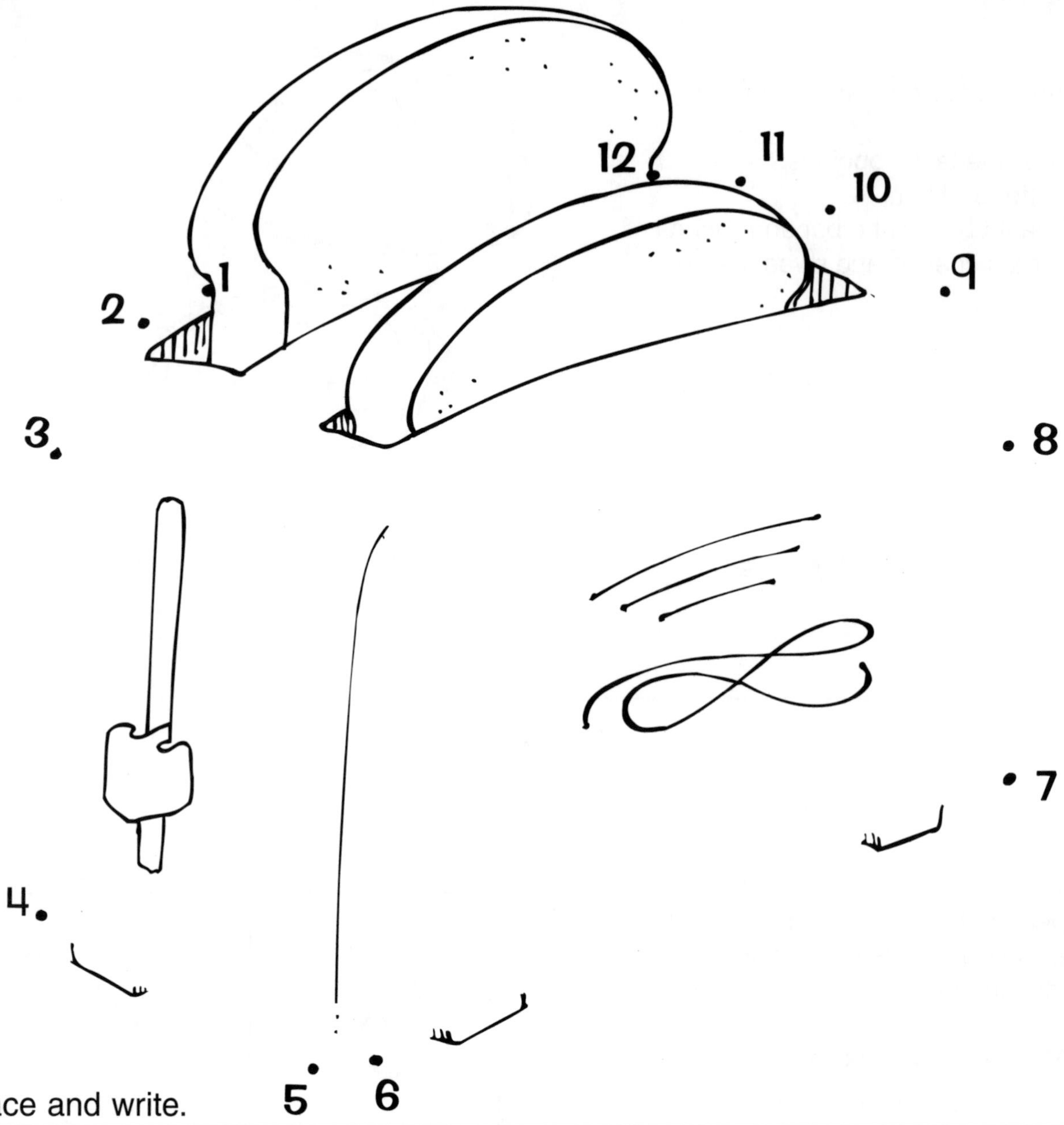

Trace and write.

t t t t t

T T T

toast

Fun with the Alphabet EMC 774

Make It! # Telephone Talk

Use this lesson as an opportunity for children to practice their own telephone number and using the telephone skills.

Materials:

- Reproduce the patterns on pages 202 and 203 on construction paper.
- scissors
- crayons
- paste
- hole punch
- 20" (51 cm) of yarn for the receiver cord
- paper fastener
- 2 paperclips

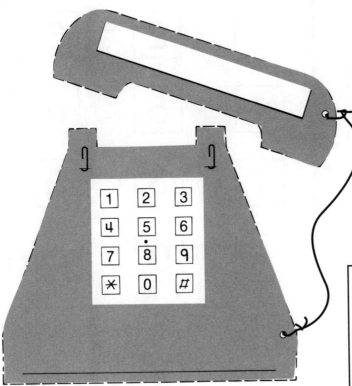

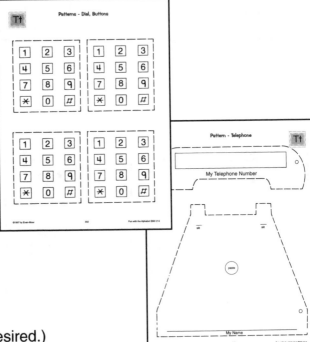

Steps to follow:

1. Cut out the telephone parts. (Color first if desired.)

2. Paste on the dial.

3. Punch holes in the receiver and the base. Tie the yarn strip through the holes.

4. Cut slits on the telephone (an adult may need to do this) and insert paper clips to hold the receiver.

 Fun with the Alphabet EMC 774

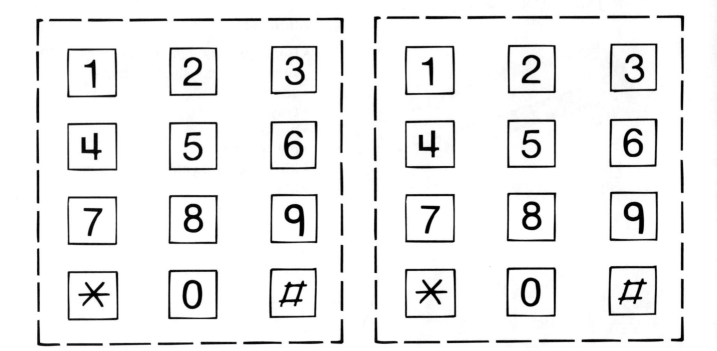

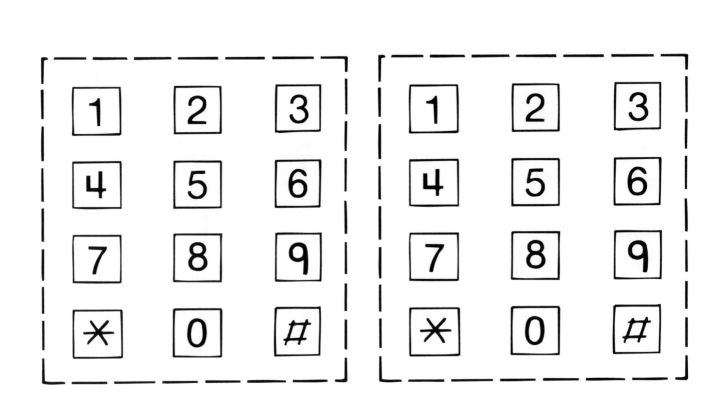

Pattern - Telephone

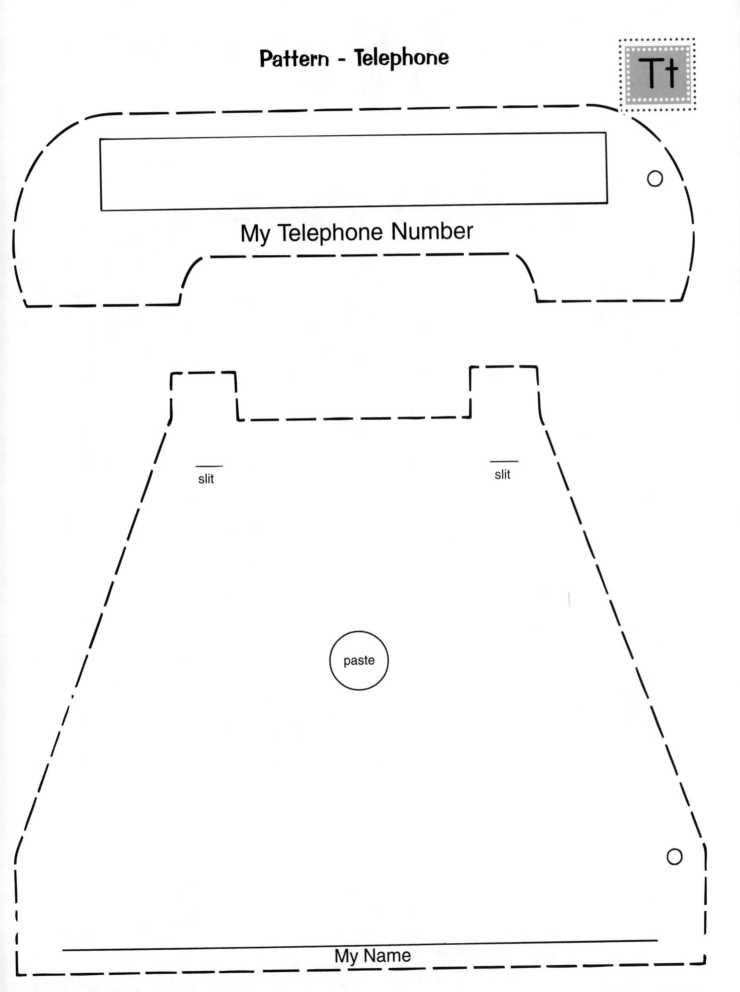

Tt

My Telephone Number

slit

slit

paste

My Name

203

Fun with the Alphabet EMC 774

In the Tent

name _____

1.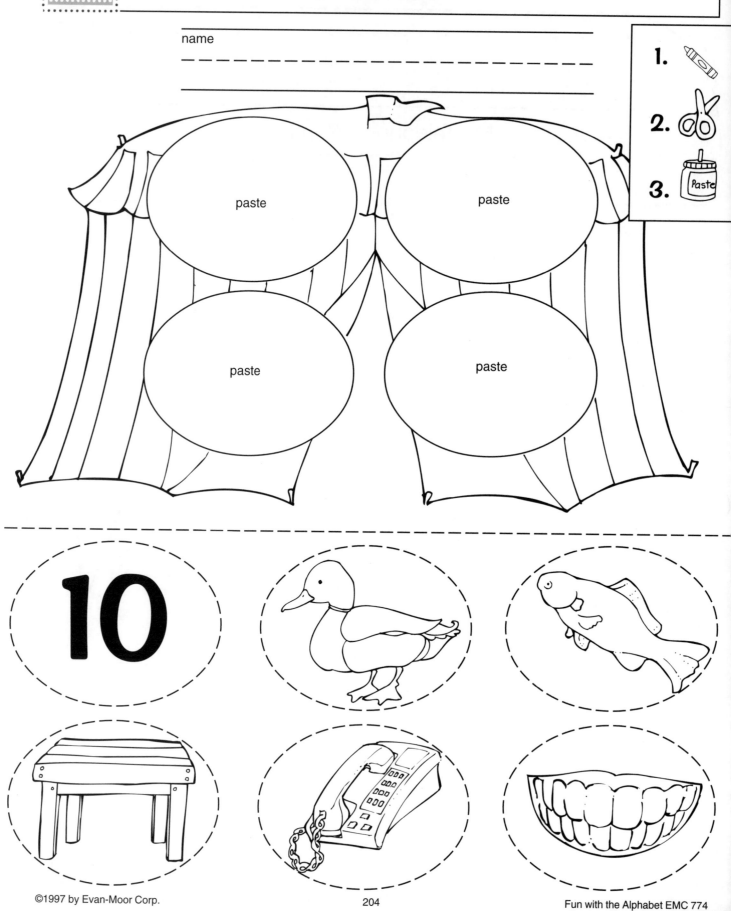
2.
3. Paste

paste

paste

paste

paste

10

204

Fun with the Alphabet EMC 774

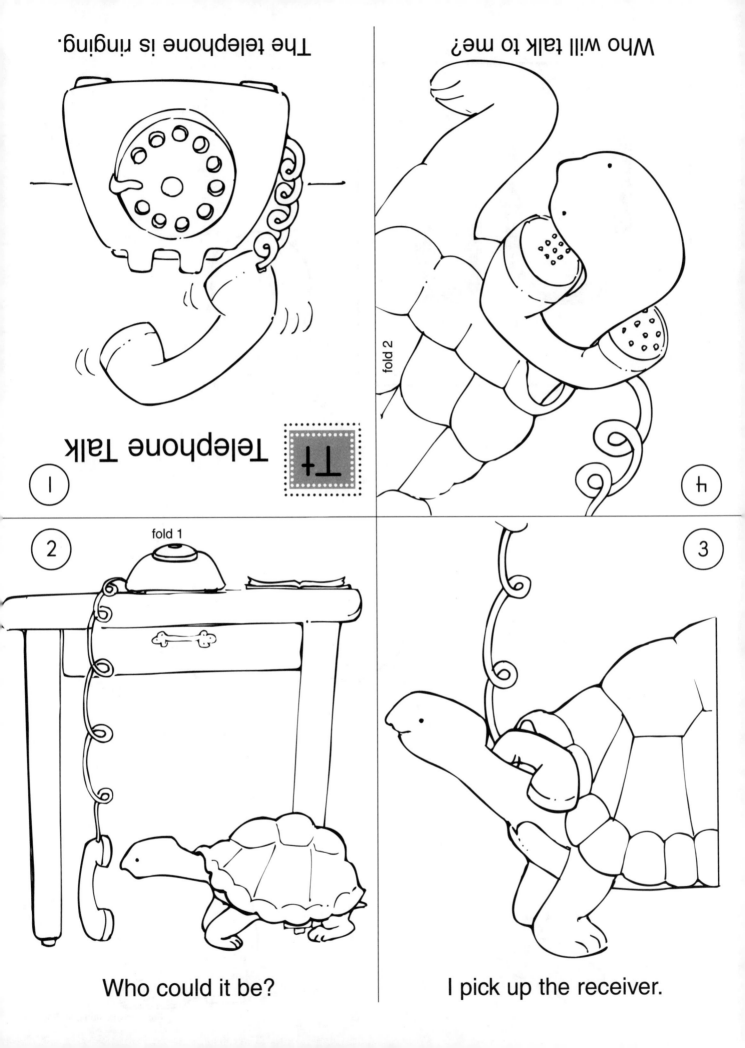

① Telephone Talk Tt
The telephone is ringing.

④ fold 2
Who will talk to me?

② fold 1
Who could it be?

③ I pick up the receiver.

Pages four and five provide teaching ideas for introducing and practicing each letter. Use these in conjunction with the specific resources for "U" listed below.

Have students sort objects. Look for real things starting with the sound "u" makes.

Note: Determine whether you will introduce both the short and long sounds of the vowel at the same time.

Alphabet Books:

Baseball ABC by Florence C. Mayer; Abrams, 1994.

Umpire's Adventure in Alphabet Land by Laura Alden; Children's Press, 1992.

Books About Umpires:

(These books contain stories about baseball in general. You will have to point out the umpire's roll.)

Albert's Ballgame by Leslie Tryon; Atheneum, 1996.

The Biggest Mouth in Baseball by Kate McMullen; Grosset & Dunlap, 1993.

Baseball (A New True Book) by Ray Brokel; Children's Press, 1982.

Baseball Ballerina by Kathryn Cristaldi; Random House, 1992.

Beginning Baseball by Julie Jensen; Lerner Publications, 1995.

Here Comes the Strikeout (An I Can Read Book) by Leonard Kessler; HarperCollins, 1965.

Books About Umbrellas:

Umbrella by Taro Yoshima; Puffin, 1977.

Umbrella Parade by Kathy Feczko; Troll (Giant First Start Reader Series), 1985.

Umbrella Thief by Sybil Wettasinghe; Kane-Miller Books, 1987.

Willow Umbrella by Christine Widman; Simon & Schuster, 1993.

Eat It!   "Unusual" Snacks

Uu

1. Spinach and peanut butter roll-ups
2. Rutabaga and turnip circles
3. Sardines and crackers
4. Rice crackers and applebutter

Let your students think up other "unusual" snacks to try.

 Draw It!   # The Umbrella

Direct students to fold a blank piece of paper into four sections. Draw on the chalkboard or use oral instructions to guide students to draw the following:

1. Make a red umbrella.

2. Make a yellow umbrella with purple polka dots.

3. Make a green umbrella in the rain.

4. Make an upside down orange umbrella.

Oral Language Experience:

Students dictate a sentence or short story about one of the pictures to an adult.

Uu

name
_____

Write It!

Color. ◌ ◌ - blue ⌂ -yellow

Draw an ☂

Trace and write.

u u u u u u

U U U U

umbrella

 **Make It!**

Umpire

This umpire is ready to make a call. Three strikes and you're out!

Materials:

- reproducible patterns (page 212)
- white paper
- black construction paper
    1 - 4 1/2" x 12" (11.5 x 30.5 cm) for body
    2 - 2" X 6" (5 x15 cm) for arms
    1 - 1/2" x 5" (1 x 13 cm) for bars on mask
- paper egg carton bottom cut in half
- paste
- scissors
- crayons
- 2 paper fasteners

Steps to follow:

1. Fold the black body paper in half. Cut up the center of the lower half.

2. Paste the egg carton to the main body part. Fold the paper at the knees.

3. Cut out all pattern pieces.

4. Color the face and hands. Draw on features with crayons.

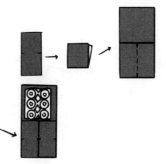

5. Paste the face piece behind the body. Overlap 2 inches (5 cm).

6. Paste the two protective facemask bars over the face. Paste only the ends so that the center forms an arch.

7. Round the top edges of the arms. Paste the hands to the arms. Attach the arms at the shoulder with paper fasteners.

 Fun with the Alphabet EMC 774

paste

Fun with the Alphabet EMC 774

Umbrella Puzzle

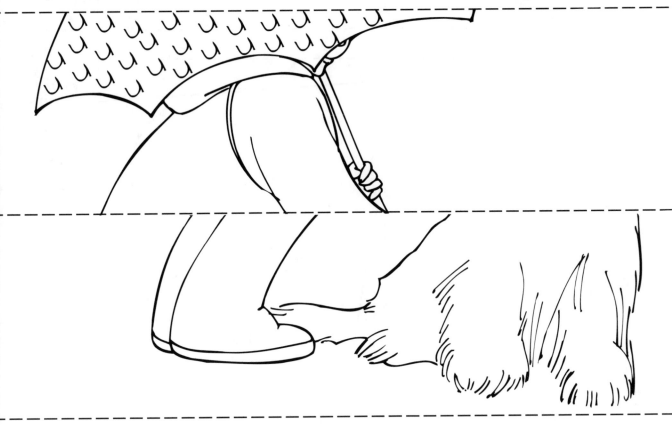

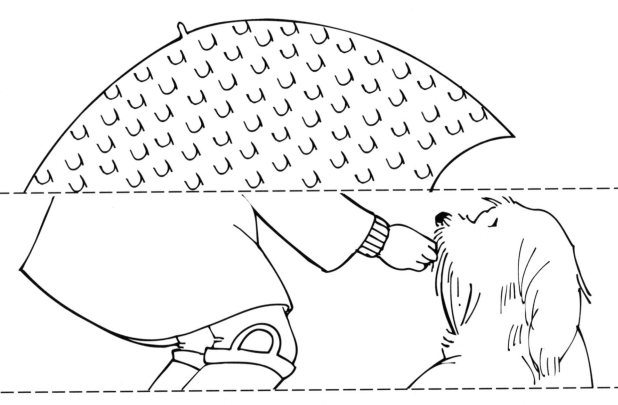

Fun with the Alphabet EMC 774

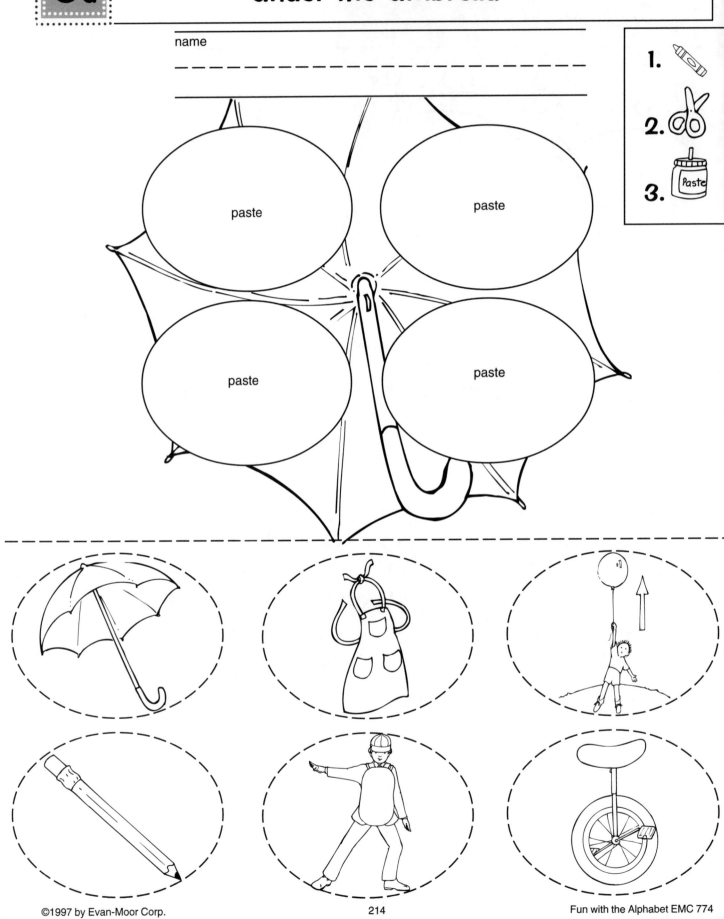

Uu

Under the Umbrella

name

1.

2.

3. Paste

paste

paste

paste

paste

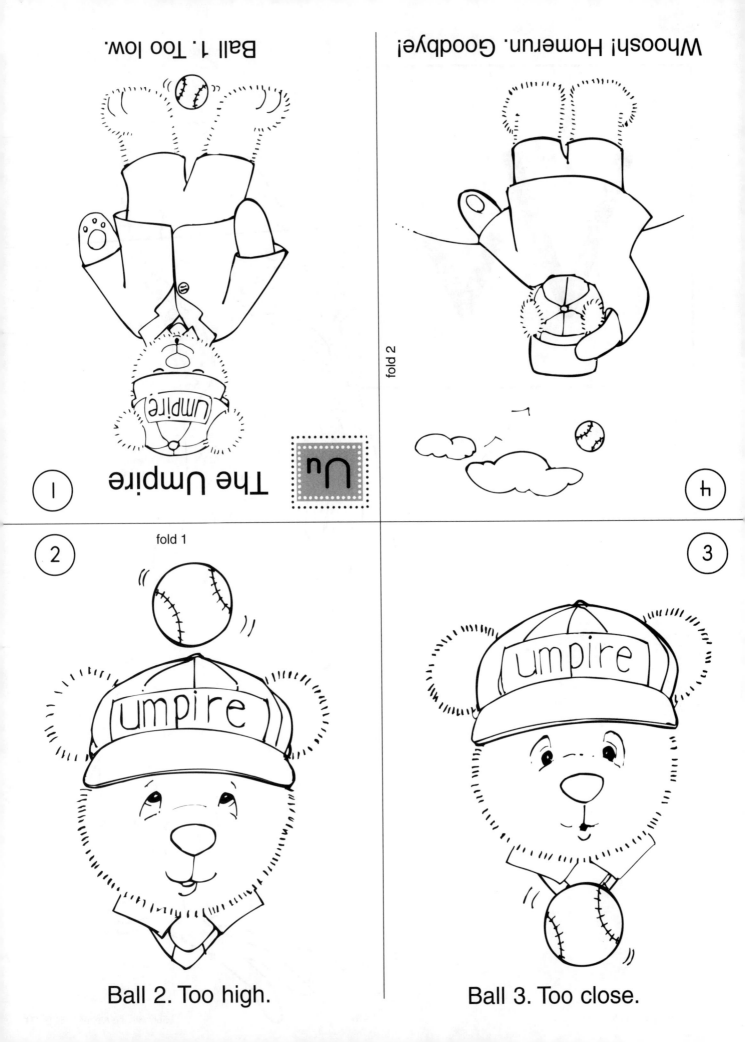

The Umpire

Uu

Ball 1. Too low.

Whoosh! Homerun. Goodbye!

fold 2

fold 1

Ball 2. Too high.

Ball 3. Too close.

V v

Pages four and five provide teaching ideas for introducing and practicing each letter. Use these in conjunction with the specific resources for "V" listed below.

Have students sort objects. Put things starting with the sound "v" makes in a wide-mouth vase.

Alphabet Books:

The Bird Alphabet Book by Jerry Pallotta; Charlesbridge, 1986.

Eating the Alphabet: Fruits and Vegetables from A to Z by Lois Ehlert; Harcourt Brace, 1989.

My First ABC by Debbie MacKinnon & Anthea Sieveking; Barron's Educational Series, Inc., 1992.

Books About Vultures:

Eli by Bill Peet; Houghton Mifflin, 1984.

Vultures by Lynn M. Stone; Carolrhoda Books, 1993.

Books About Vans and Other Vehicles:

Cars and Trucks and Things That Go by Richard Scarry; Golden Press, 1974.

Wheels Around by Shelly Rotner; Houghton Mifflin, 1995.

William the Vehicle King by Laura P. Newton; Bradbury Press, 1987.

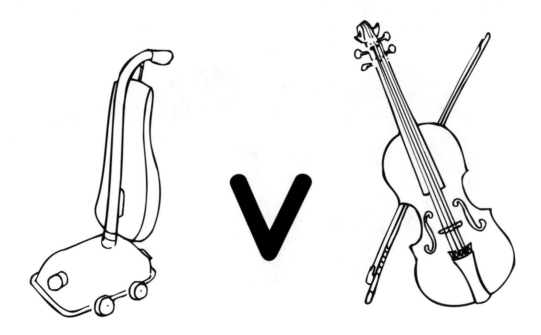

Eat It! # Very Vegetable Soup

- 4 quarts (1 liter) chicken or beef broth
- 1 chopped onion (optional)
- 6 sliced carrots
- 6 sliced celery stalks
- 2 small cans tomatoes
- 6 cubed potatoes
- 1 package frozen corn
- pepper and salt to taste
- 1 bay leaf

1. Put all ingredients in a soup pot.

2. Simmer until "veggies" are tender.

3. Remove bay leaf before serving.

 Draw It! # The Van

Direct students to fold a blank piece of paper into four sections. Draw on the chalkboard and use oral instructions to guide students to draw the following:

1. Make an orange van on the road.

2. Make a red van on the grass.

3. Make a green van going down hill.

4. Make a blue van going uphill.

Oral Language Experience:

Students dictate a sentence or short story about one of the pictures to an adult.

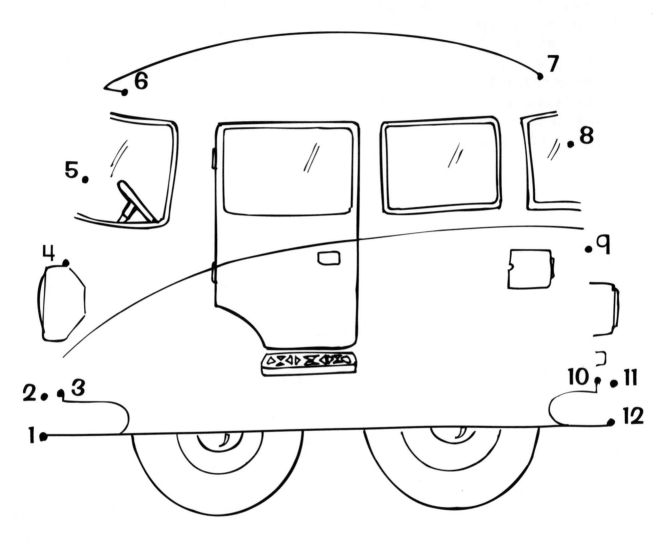

Trace and write.

V V V V V V

V V V V V

van

This vulture is ready to perch on your desk or a friend's shoulder.

Materials:

- reproducible patterns on pages 222 and 223
- white construction paper
- craft stick
- tape
- paste
- crayons
- scissors

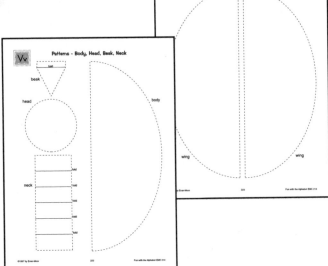

Steps to follow:

1. Color and cut out the pattern pieces.

   body, wings - black
   head and neck - red
   beak - yellow

2. Paste the wings and body together. Bend the wings down.

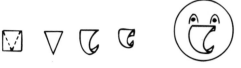

3. Make the head:

   Curl the tip of the beak on a pencil.
   Fold along the fold line and paste the beak to the head.
   Add eyes with a black crayon.

4. Make the neck:

   Accordian fold the red neck piece.
   Paste one end of this strip to the main body piece.
   Paste the other end to the head.

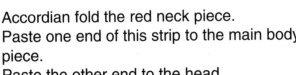

5. Attach a tongue depressor handle to the back of the main body piece with tape.

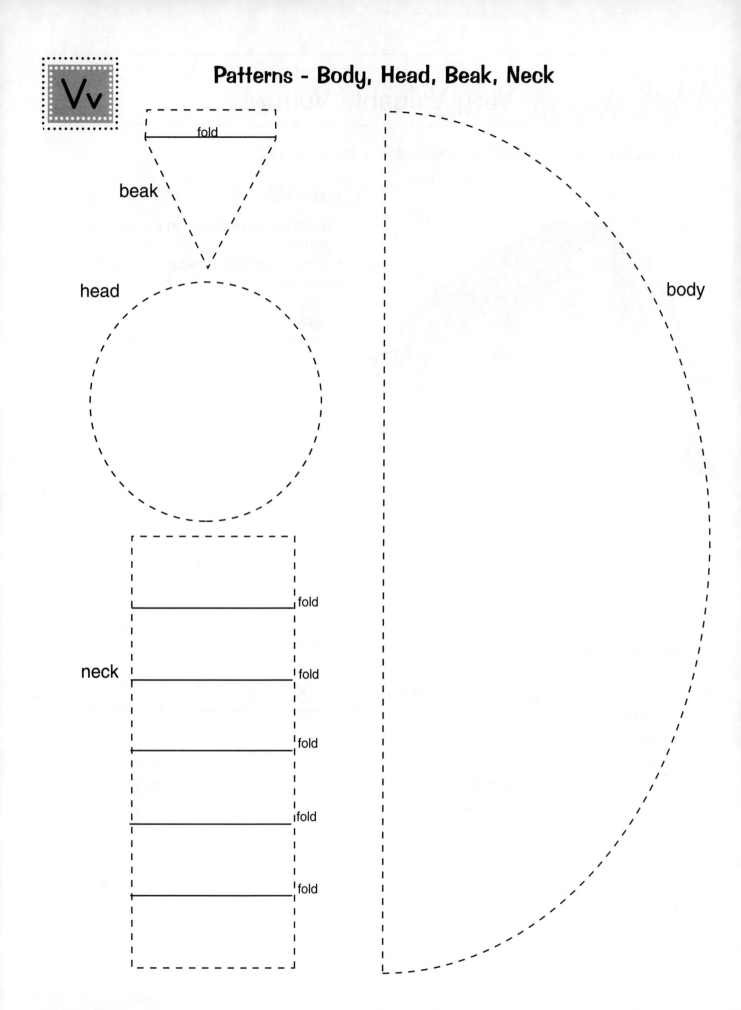

Patterns - Body, Head, Beak, Neck

beak

head

neck

fold

fold

fold

fold

fold

fold

body

Fun with the Alphabet EMC 774

Patterns - Wings

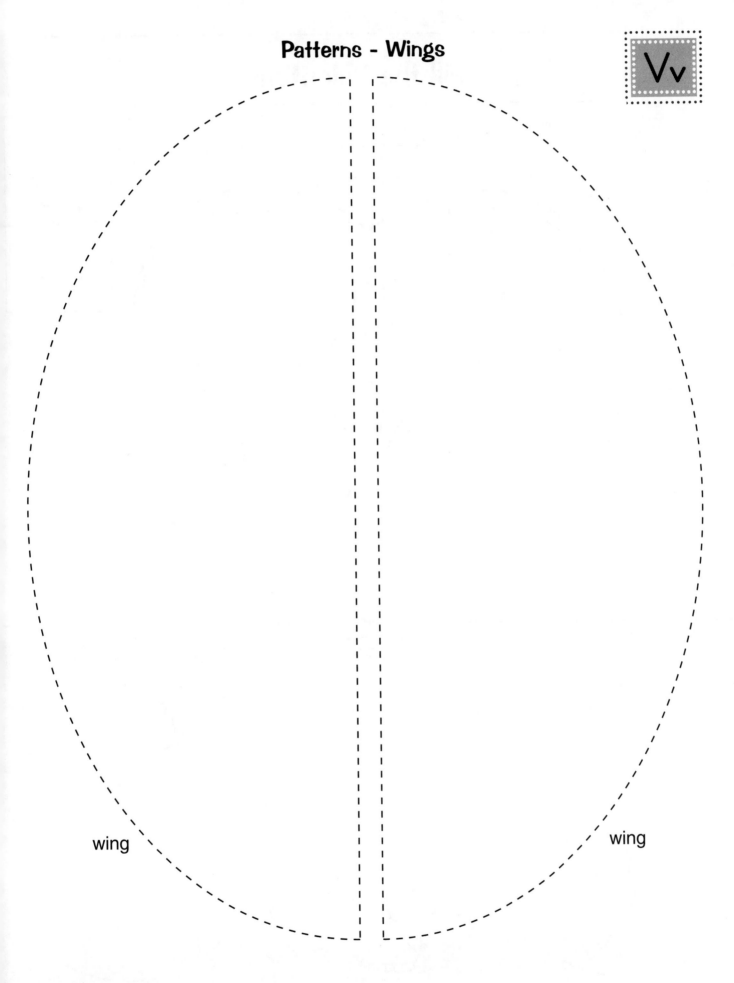

wing

wing

Fun with the Alphabet EMC 774

Fill the Valentine

name

1.

2.

3.

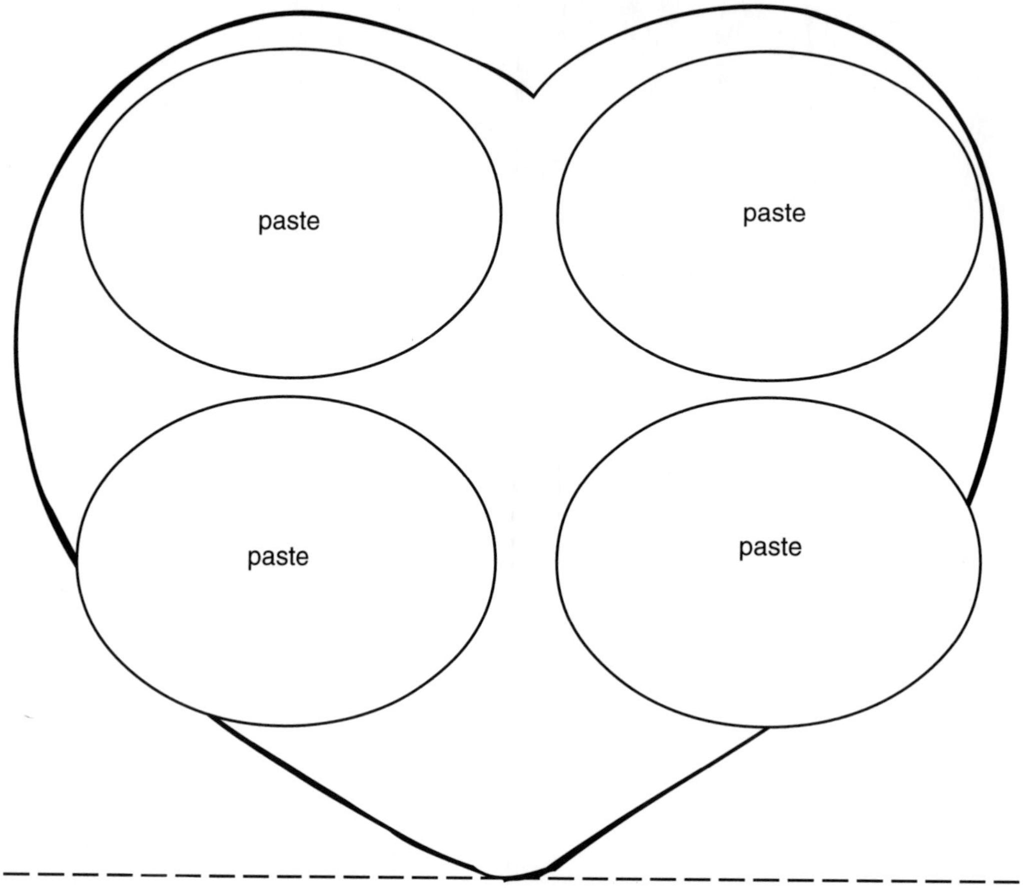

paste

paste

paste

paste

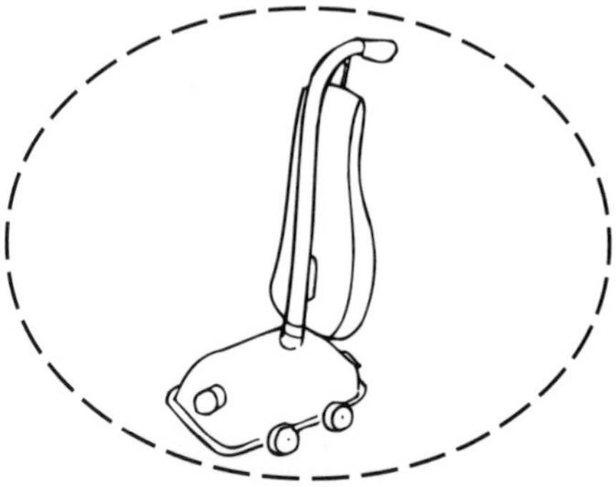

Vinney needs a friend.

3

Vinney is so sad.

2

fold 1

4

visit a vulture

A vulture's not so bad.

Vv   Vinney Vulture

1

fold 2

Vinney Vulture is lonely.

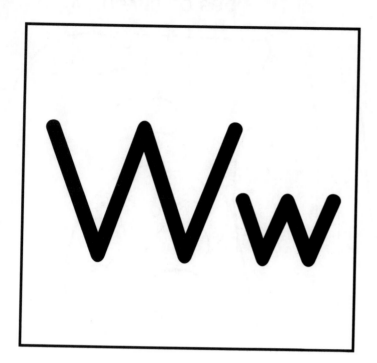

 **Learn It!**

Teaching the Letter

Pages four and five provide teaching ideas for introducing and practicing each letter. Use these in conjunction with the specific resources for "W" listed below.

Have students sort objects. Put things starting with the sound "w" makes in a wagon.

Fun with the Alphabet EMC 774

Alphabet Books:

A Bold Carnivore: An Alphabet of Predators by Consie Powell; Roberts, 1995.

A Caribou Alphabet by Mary Beth Owens; Dog Ear Press, 1988.

The Wildlife ABC: A Nature Alphabet Book by Jan Thornhill; Simon & Schuster, 1990.

Books About Walruses:

A First Look at Seals, Sea Lions, and Walruses (A First Look At Series) by Millicent Ellis Selsam; Walker, 1988.

Here is the Arctic Winter by Madeleine Dunphy; Hyperion Books for Children, 1993.

Walpole by Syd Hoff; Harper & Row, 1977.

Walrus by Kathy Darling; Lothrop, Lee & Shepard, 1991.

Walruses (Sea Mammal Discovery Library) by S. Palmer; Rourke, 1989.

Books About Wagons:

The Box with Red Wheels by Maud and Miska Petersham; Aladdin Paperbacks (Simon & Schuster), 1986.

Sam's Wagon by Barbro Lindgren; Morrow, 1986.

Skip to My Lou by Nadine Westcott; Little, Brown, 1992.

Wonderful Waffles

Use frozen waffles or make up your favorite recipe. Top with syrup and butter or whipped cream and fresh fruit.

 Draw It! **Wagons**

Direct students to fold a blank piece of paper into four sections. Draw on the chalkboard and use oral instructions to guide students to draw the following:

1. Make a red wagon on the grass.

2. Make a red wagon rolling downhill.

3. Make a green ball in a purple wagon.

4. Make a surprise wagon. Make it colorful.

Oral Language Experience:

Students dictate a sentence or short story about one of the pictures to an adult.

Draw a web in the window.

Trace and write.

W W W W W

W W W

web window

Willy Walrus

This walrus is swimming in the icy waters looking for his lunch.

Materials:

- blue construction paper for the background 9" x 12" (23 x 30.5 cm)
- patterns on page 232
- drinking straw
- crayons
- scissors
- paste
- razor blade or mat knife (adult use only)
- stapler

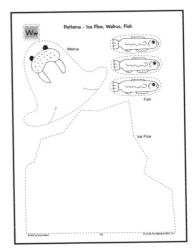

Steps to follow:

1. Fold up about 3" (7.5 cm) on the bottom of the blue paper.

2. Make a 1" (2.5 cm) slit in the fold line. (This must be done by an adult.)

3. Cut a wave line along the bottom. Staple the flap up.

4. Color and cut out the pattern pieces:

   ice floe - white
   walrus - brown
   fish - any color

5. Paste the ice floe to the blue paper.

6. Tape the straw to the back of the walrus. Slip the straw through the slit in the fold line of the blue paper.

7. Paste the fish in the water.

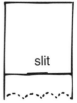

Fun with the Alphabet EMC 774

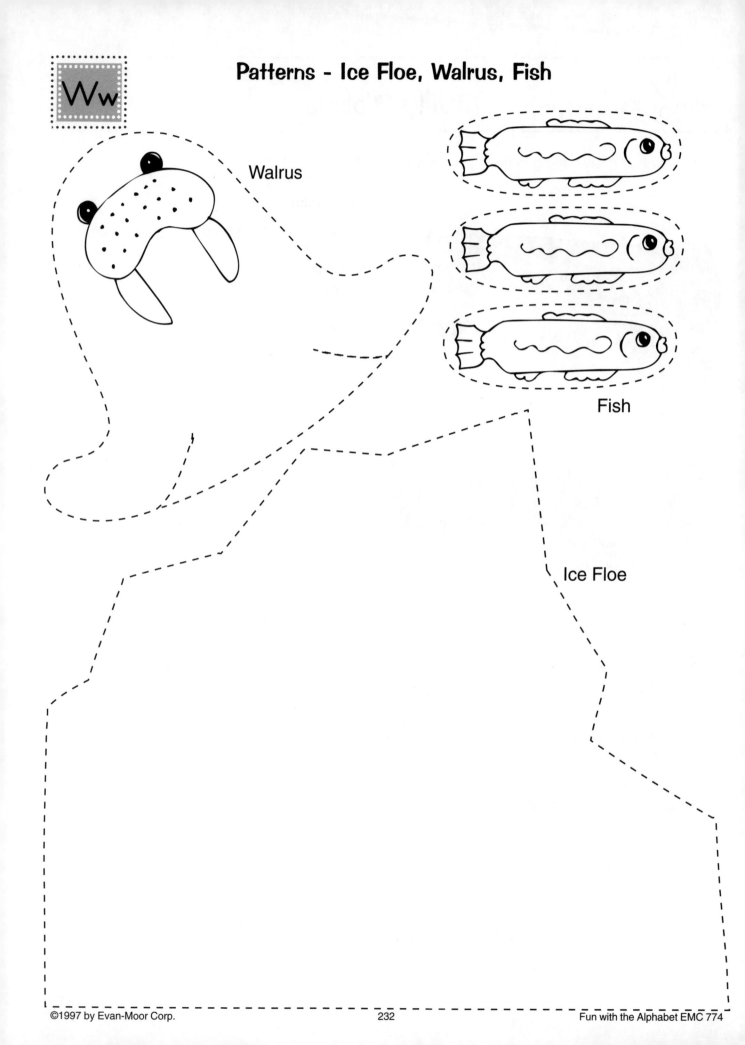

Patterns - Ice Floe, Walrus, Fish

Ww

Walrus

Fish

Ice Floe

What Is Hidden Here?

Can you find these pictures?
walrus   wagon   well   wig   web   window

Ride the Wave

name

paste

paste

paste

paste

1.

2.

3. Paste

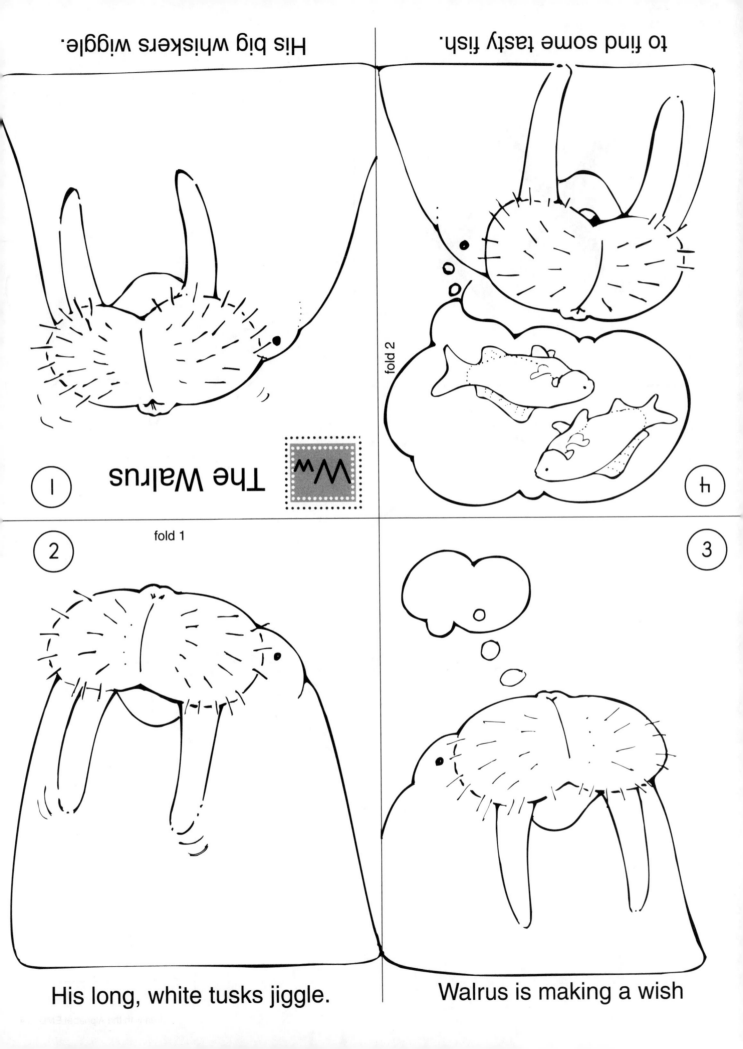

The Walrus

His big whiskers wiggle.

to find some tasty fish.

His long, white tusks jiggle.

Walrus is making a wish

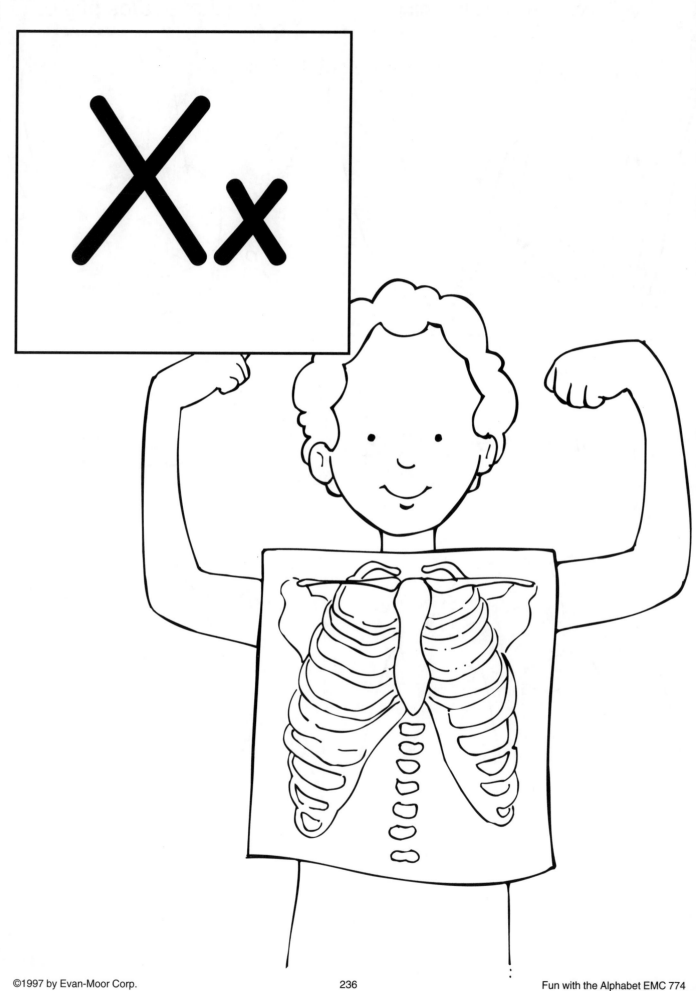

 **Learn It!** # Teaching the Letter

Pages four and five provide teaching ideas for introducing and practicing each letter.
Use these in conjunction with the specific resources for "X" listed below.

Have students sort objects. Put things starting or ending with the sound "x" makes in a box.

Alphabet Books:

Alphabet City by Stephen Johnson; Viking, 1995.

Animal Alphabet by Ben Kitchen; Viking, 1992.

What's Your Name? From Ariel to Zoe by Eve Sanders; Holiday House, 1995.

Wildlife ABC: A Nature Alphabet by Jan Thornhill; Simon & Schuster, 1990.

Books About Foxes:

Amazing Wolves, Dogs, and Foxes (Eyewitness Junior) by Mary Ling; Knopf, 1991.

Arctic Foxes by Downs Matthews; Simon & Schuster, 1995.

The Cat and the Rooster: A Ukranian Folktale by Ivan Malkovych; Knopf, 1995.

Down by the Road by Margrit Cruickshank; Simon & Schuster, 1995.

Hattie and the Fox by Mem Fox; Bradbury Press, 1987.

Rosie's Walk by Pat Hutchins; Macmillan, 1968.

Wings: A Tale of Two Chickens by James Marshall; Viking, 1995.

Books About Other Things That Have an "X."

The Skeleton Inside You (Let's Read and Find Out Science Series) by Philip Balestrino; Crowell, 1989.

Sitting in My Box by Dee Lillegard; Dutton, 1989.

Six Busy Days by Mary Erickson; Chariot Books, 1988.

Six Crows by Leo Lionni; Knopf, 1988.

Webster and Arnold and the Giant Box by Patricia K. Roche; Dial Press, 1980.

X marks the top of these delicious buns. Buy hot cross buns at the bakery. Children can add a more definite X using frosting. (Get the kind you squeeze out of little tubes.)

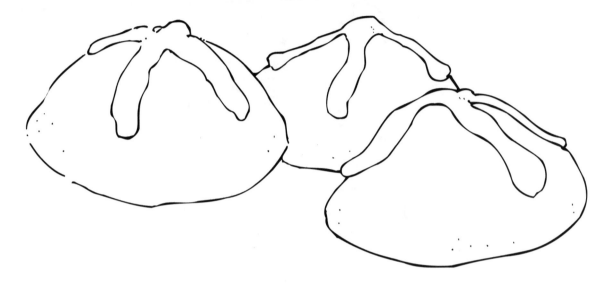

 Draw It!   # Red Xs

Direct students to fold a blank piece of paper into four sections. Draw on the chalkboard and use oral instructions to guide students to draw the following:

1. Make an ax with a red handle.

2. Make a box of red balls.

3. Make a red jack-in-the-box.

4. Make a red fox.

Oral Language Experience:

Students dictate a sentence or short story about one of the pictures to an adult.

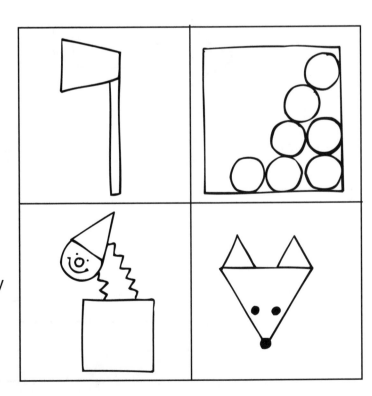

name

Write It!

Color.

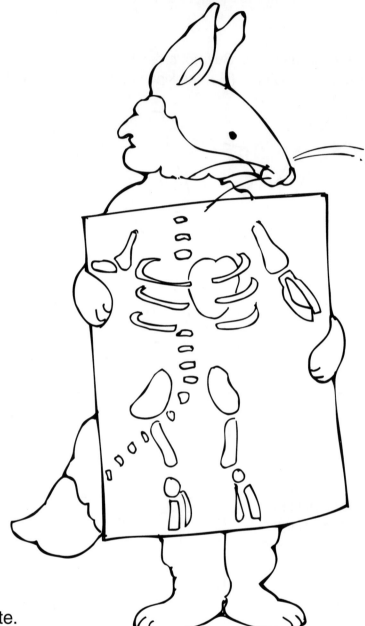

Trace and write.

X X X X X

X X X X X

fox x-ray

Make It! A Foxy Loxy Headband

This little fox is fun to wear while listening to stories about things that contain an "x" or reciting fox poems.

Materials:

- reproducible patterns (pages 242 and 243)
- white paper
- 2- 12" x 3" (30.5 x 7.5 cm) white strips of construction paper pasted together to form the headband
- crayons
- glue
- stapler

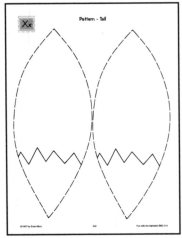

Steps to follow:

1. Color all the pattern parts (fox's face red; tail red with a white tip).
2. Cut out all the pieces.
3. Fold the head on the marked lines.
4. Staple the headband to fit each child's head.
5. Paste the head and tail pieces to the headband.

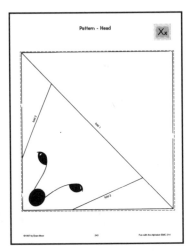

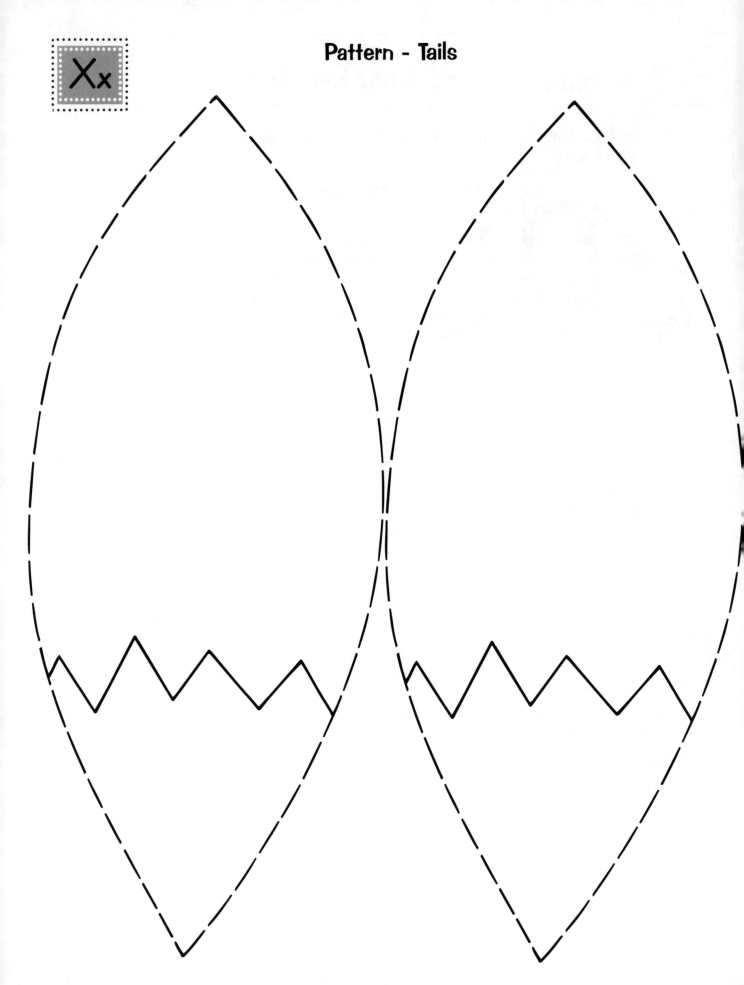

Fun with the Alphabet EMC 774

Pattern - Head

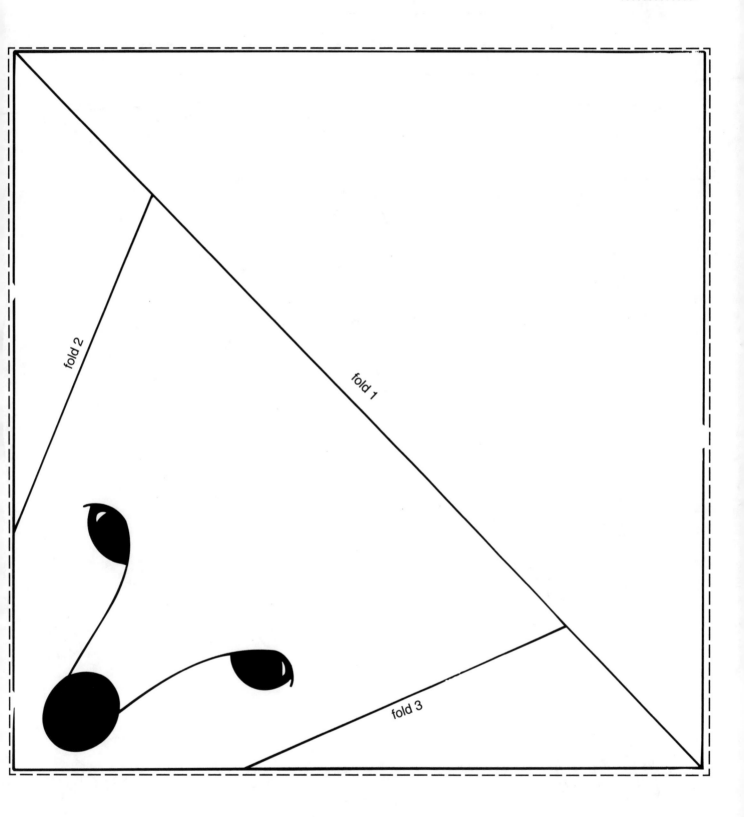

fold 2

fold 1

fold 3

Find the "X" Words

1.
2.
3. Paste

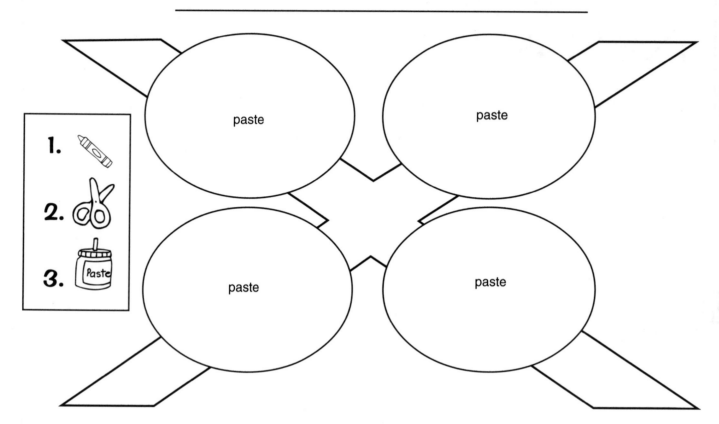

paste   paste

paste   paste

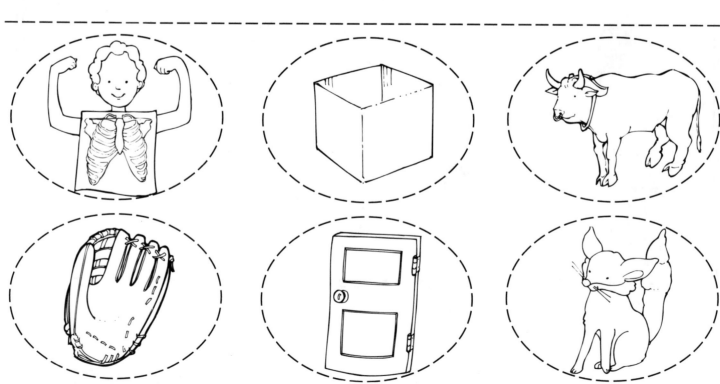

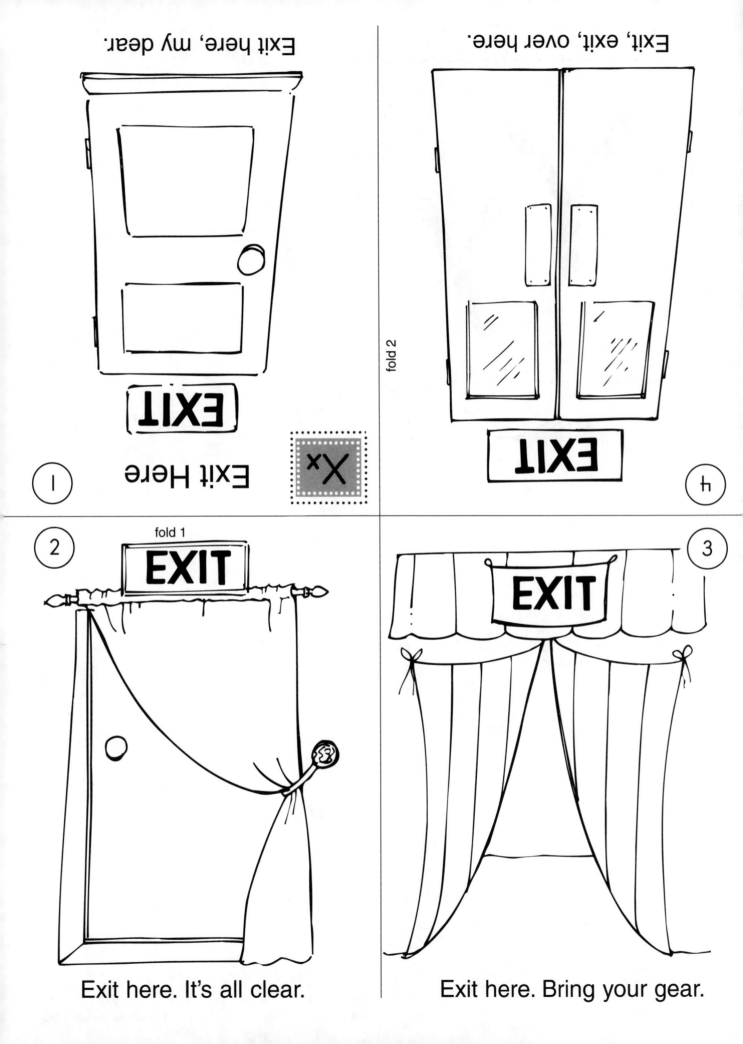

Exit here, my dear.

Exit Here

EXIT

①

fold 2

Exit, exit, over here.

EXIT

4

fold 1

EXIT

②

Exit here. It's all clear.

EXIT

③

Exit here. Bring your gear.

246

Pages four and five provide teaching ideas for introducing and practicing each letter. Use these in conjunction with the specific resources for "Y" listed below.

Have students sort objects. Find real things starting with the sound "y" makes.

Alphabet Books:

All in the Woodland Early, An ABC Book by Jane Yolen; Boyds Mill Press, 1991.

A, My Name is Alice by Jane Bayer; Dial Books for Young Readers, 1984.

It Begins With an A by Stephanie Calmenson; Hyperion, 1994.

Books About "Yankee Doodle Dandies":

Yankee Doodle by Edward Bangs; Four Winds Press, 1984.

Yankee Doodle by Gary Chalk; Dorling Kindersley, 1993.

Books About "Yo" and Yo-Yos:

Tops: Experimenting With Spinning Toys by Bernie Zubrowski; Morrow Junior Books, 1989. (Use appropriate pages.)

Yo, Hungry Wolf by David Vozar; Doubleday, 1993.

Yo! Yes? by Chris Raschka; Orchard Books, 1993.

Eat It! # Yummy Yellow Yogurt

Have several flavors available for sampling in addition to lemon. Be sure to include plain yogurt. Play a tasting game. Blindfold a volunteer. Have the child taste all the kinds trying to find the "yummy yellow" one.

 **Draw It!** # Yo-Yo

Direct students to fold a blank piece of paper into four sections. Draw on the chalkboard and use oral instructions to guide students to draw the following:

1. Make a purple yo-yo.

2. Make a little blue yo-yo.

3. Make a spinning green yo-yo.

4. Make a surprise yo-yo. Make it colorful.

Oral Language Experience:

Students dictate a sentence or short story about one of the pictures to an adult.

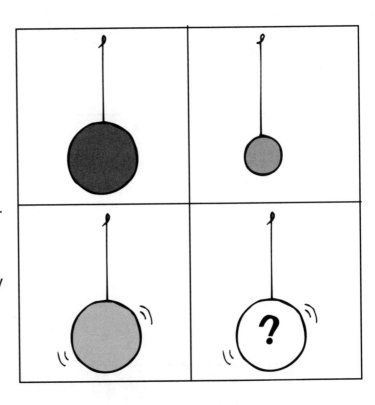

 Fun with the Alphabet EMC 774

Yy

 **Write It!**

Color.

Trace and write.

y y y y y

Y Y Y Y Y

yo-yo yak

Fun with the Alphabet EMC 774

Wear this hat and march around the room as you sing "Yankee Doodle." Select someone to carry the flag as you march and sing.

Materials:

- reproducible patterns on page 252
- 1 - double sheet of newspaper trimmed down to a square.
- scraps of construction paper (to use in decorating hats)
- paste
- crayons

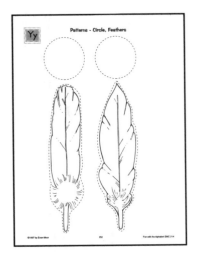

Steps to follow:

1. Fold the newspaper square.

2. Paste the loose flaps to the main section of the hat.

3. Color the circle and feather patterns. Cut out the pieces and paste them to the hat.

4. Crayons may be used to add polka dots, stripes, etc.

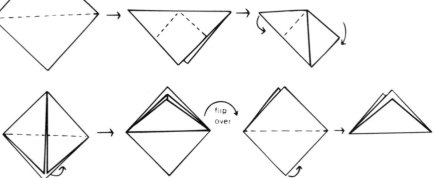

Patterns - Circles, Feathers

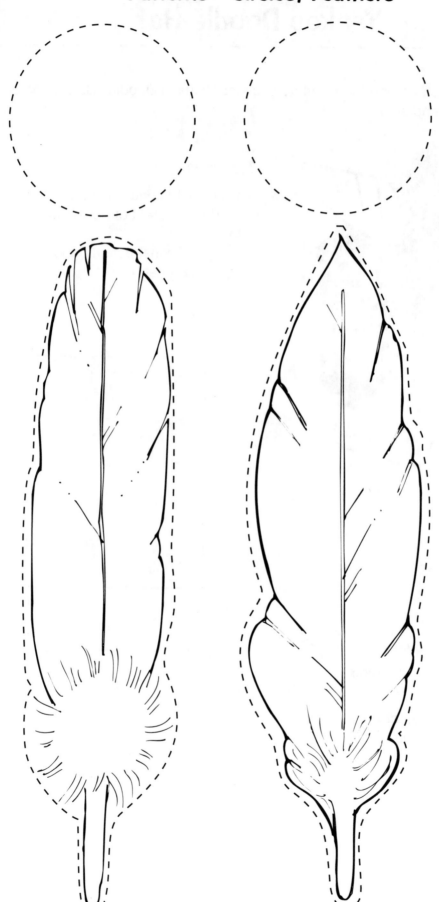

Fun with the Alphabet EMC 774

Yo-Yo Puzzle

Yum! What's Cooking?

name

1.

2.

3. Paste

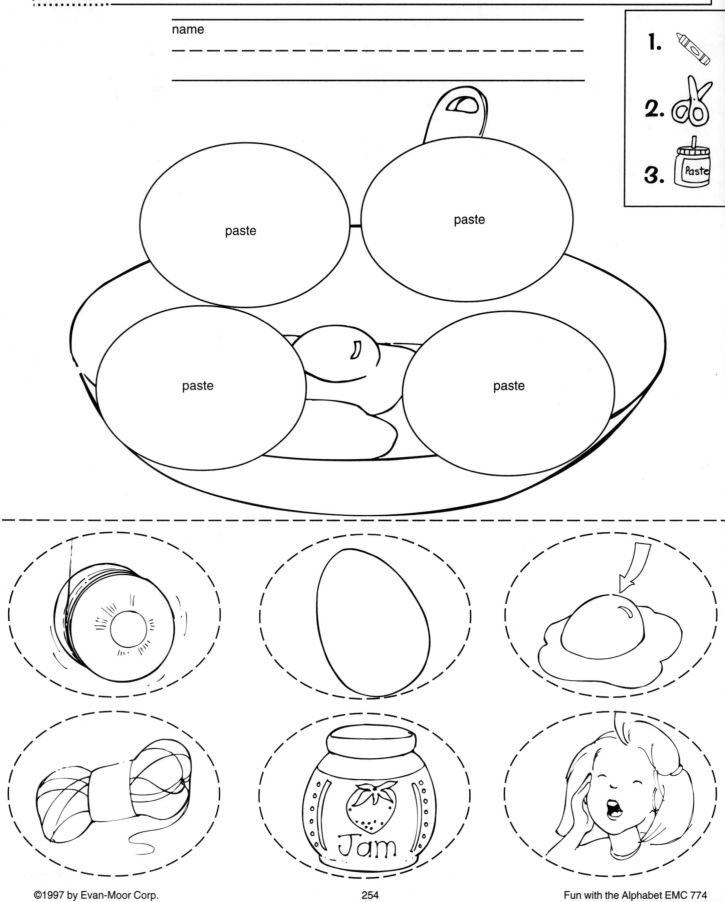

paste

paste

paste

paste

Fun with the Alphabet EMC 774

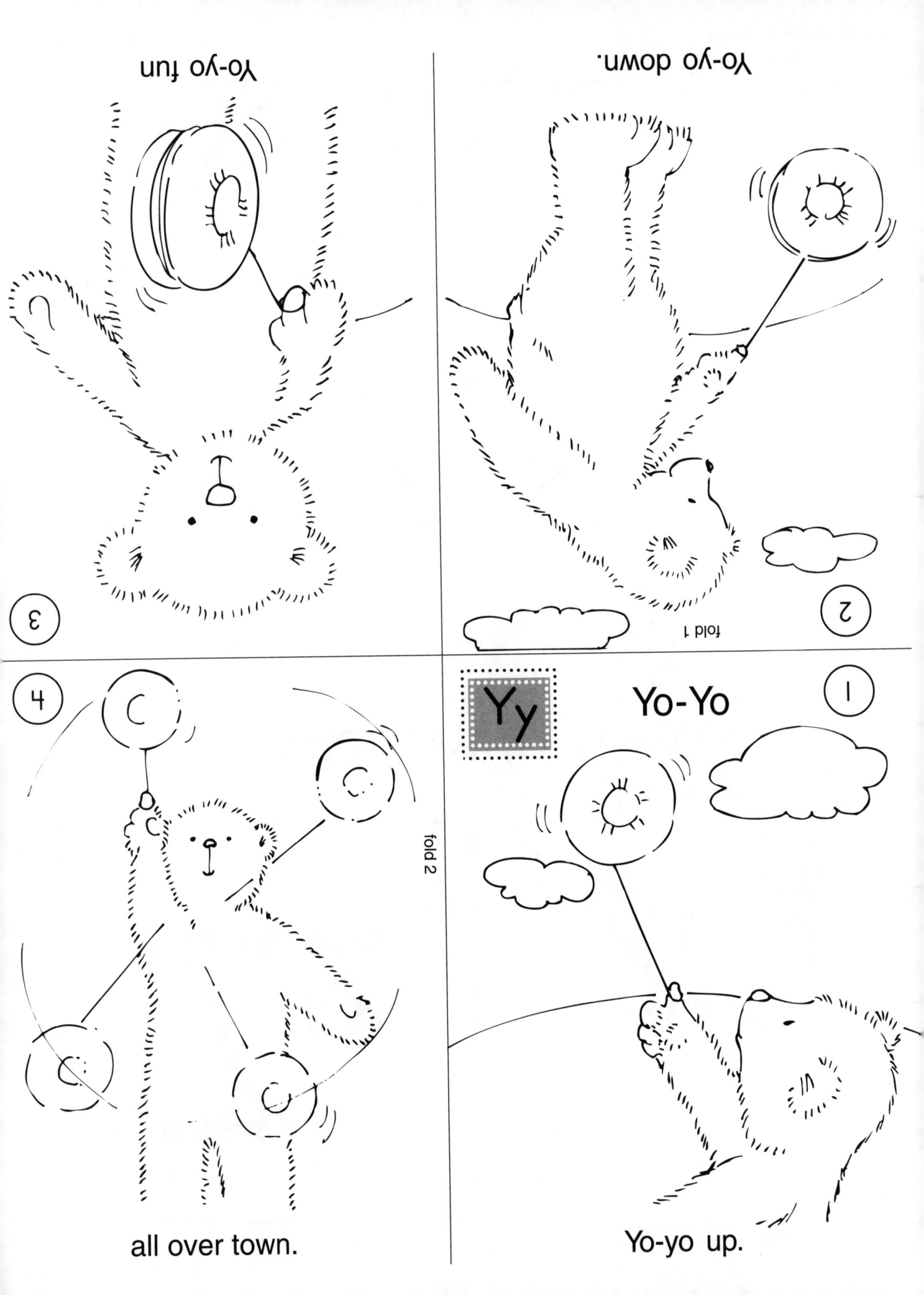

Yo-Yo

Yy

1

Yo-yo up.

Yo-yo down.

fold 1

2

3

Yo-yo fun

fold 2

4

all over town.

256

Fun with the Alphabet EMC 774

Pages four and five provide teaching ideas for introducing and practicing each letter. Use these in conjunction with the specific resources for "Z" listed below.

Have students sort objects. Find things or pictures starting with the sound "z" makes.

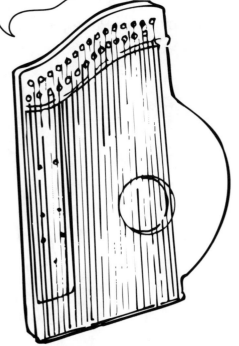

Alphabet Books:

Allison's Zinnias by Anita Lobel; Greenwillow Books, 1990.

Alphabeasts: A Hide and Seek Alphabet Book by Durga Bernhard; Holiday House, 1993.

African Animals by Philippa-Alys Browne; Sierra, 1995.

Books About Zebras:

Za-Za's Baby Brother by Lucy Cousins; Candlewick Press, 1995.

Zebra by Mary Hoffman; Raintree Steck Vaughn, 1985.

Zebras by Emilie U. Lepthien; Children's Press, 1994.

Zebra's Hiccups by David McKee; Simon & Schuster, 1993.

Zella, Zack and Zodiac by Bill Peet; Houghton Mifflin, 1986.

Greedy Zebra by Mwenye Hadithi; Little, Brown, 1984.

Books About Other "Z" Things:

Mrs. Toggle's Zipper by Robin Pulver; Four Winds Press, 1990.

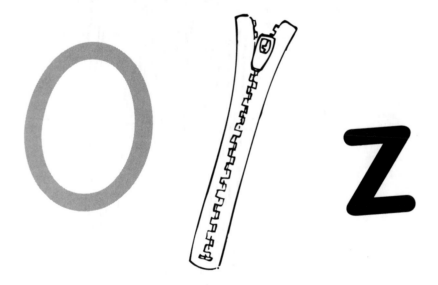

- Zucchini spears
- Dip

Prepare a package of your favorite vegetable dip. Chill and serve with the zucchini spears.

 Draw It! **Zigzag**

Direct students to fold a blank piece of paper into four sections. Draw on the chalkboard and use oral instructions to guide students to draw the following:

1. Make a zigzag across the box. Color it green.

2. Make a zigzag down the box. It looks like lightning in the sky. Make the sky blue.

3. Make a zigzag for a mouth. The boy looks unhappy.

4. Make a zigzag for a zipper.

Oral Language Experience:

Students dictate a sentence or short story about one of the pictures to an adult.

Zz

 **Write It!**

Color stripes on the zebra.

Trace and write.

z z z z z z

Z Z Z Z Z Z

zebra

The zebra's stripes appear in many variations so children may freely create their own designs.

Materials:

- reproducible pattern on page 262
- 1 - 9" x 12" (23 x 30.5 cm) white construction paper (for body)
- 8" (20 cm) strip of black yarn for a tail (knot both ends)
  - crayons
  - paste

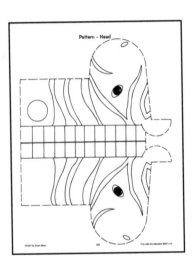

Steps to follow:

1. Fold the white construction paper in half. Hold the fold while cutting a half circle from the open side.

2. Draw and color zebra stripes on both sides of the body piece.

3. Color the stripes on the head pattern and cut it out. Fold on the fold line, and paste the head together.

4. Paste the finished head to one side of the zebra's body (inside).

5. Paste the knotted yarn tail inside the other end.

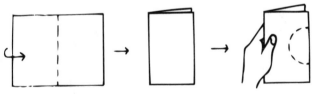

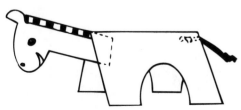

Pattern - Head

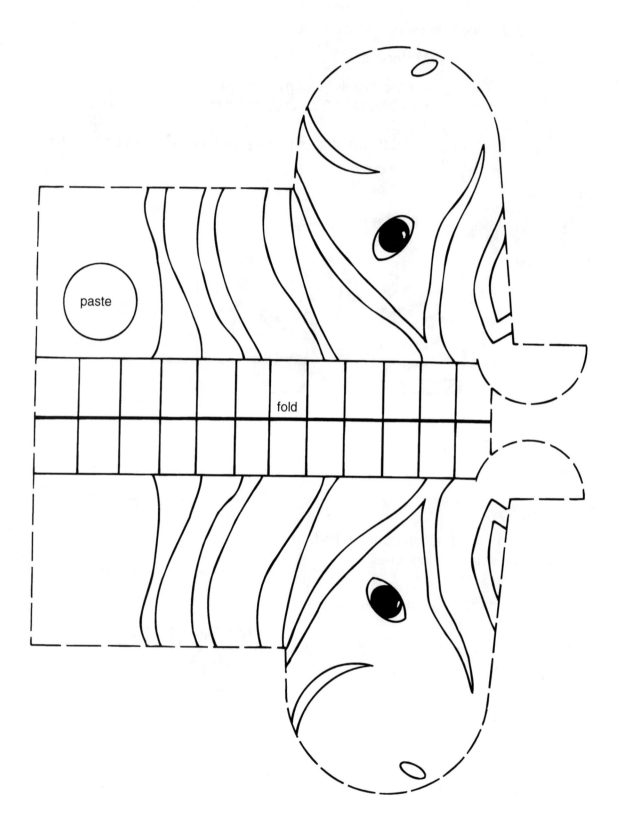

paste

fold

262

Fun with the Alphabet EMC 774

Hidden Picture

Can you find the zebra?

263

Fun with the Alphabet EMC 774

On a Zigzag

1.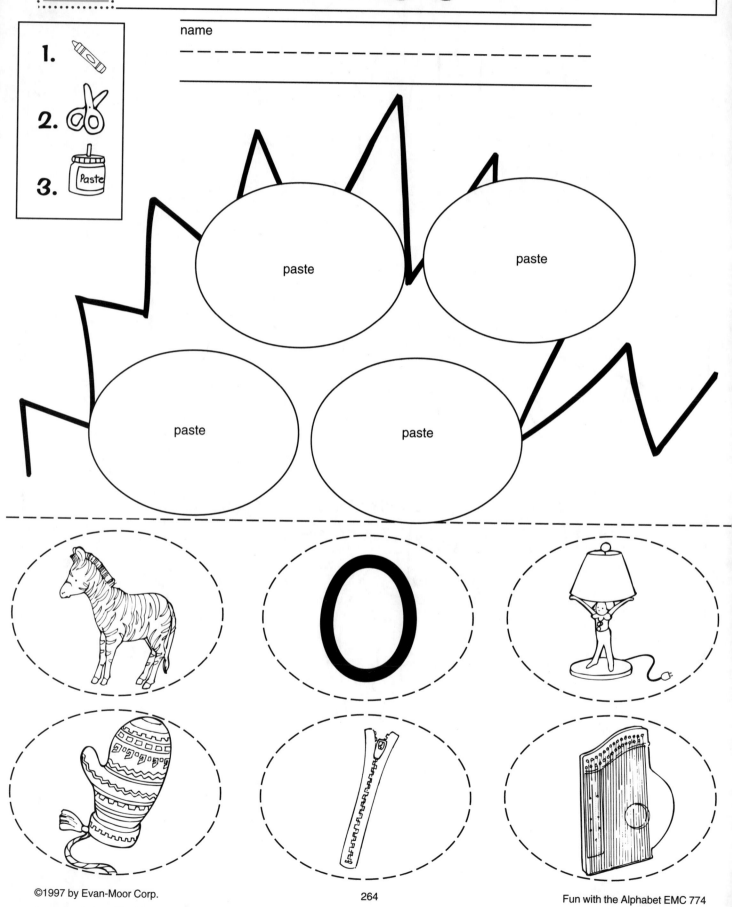

2.

3. Paste

name

paste

paste

paste

paste

1

The Zebra

Zz

Zebra has black and white stripes.

fold 1

fold 2

4

across the African plain.

2

Zebra has hooves and a mane.

3

Zebra grazes on grass

Directions:

1. Reproduce pages 266 – 272

2. Color and cut the pages apart.

3. Staple together in ABC order.

4. Put tape over the staples.

5. Read the book together.

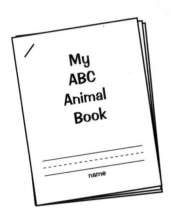

My ABC Animal Book

_____

‑ ‑ ‑ ‑ ‑ ‑ ‑ ‑ ‑ ‑ ‑ ‑ ‑ ‑ ‑ ‑

_____

name

Aa

A is for ant.

Bb

B is for bee.

Fun with the Alphabet EMC 774

Cc

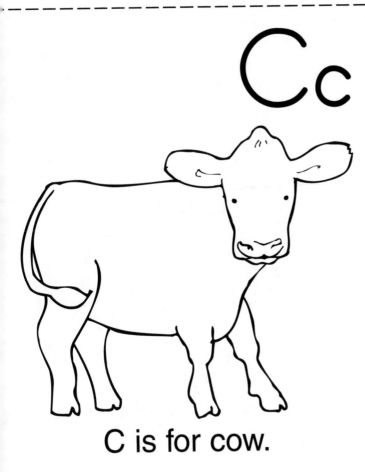

C is for cow.

Dd

D is for dinosaur.

Ee

E is for eagle.

Ff

F is for fish.

Fun with the Alphabet EMC 774

Gg

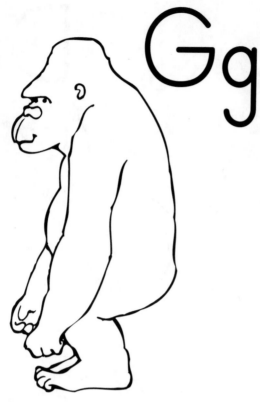

G is for gorilla.

Hh

H is for hen.

I i

I is for iguana.

Jj

J is for jellyfish.

Kk

K is for kangaroo.

Ll

L is for lion.

Mm

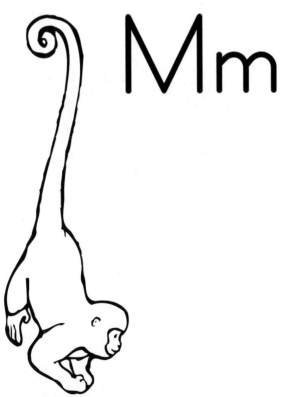

M is for monkey.

Nn

N is for newt.

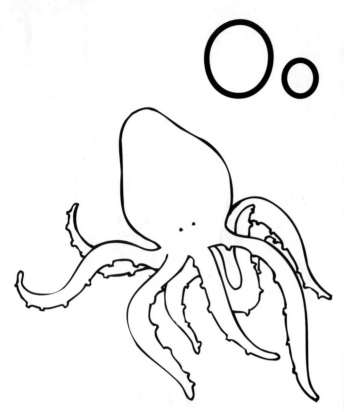

Oo

O is for octopus.

Pp

P is for pig.

Qq

Q is for quail.

Rr

R is for rabbit.

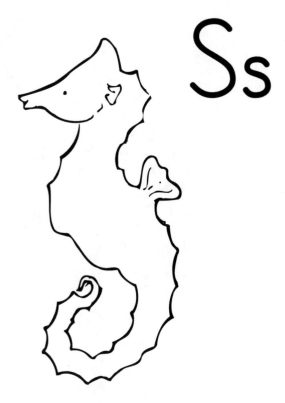

Ss

S is for seahorse.

Tt

T is for turtle.

Uu

U is for umbrella bird.

Vv

V is for vulture.

Fun with the Alphabet EMC 774

Ww

W is for walrus.

Xx

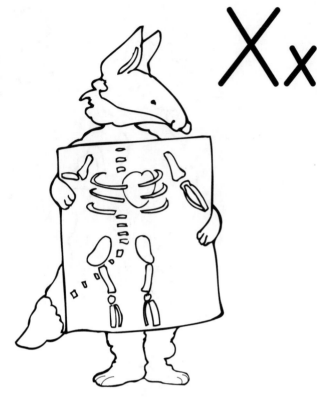

X is for x-ray of a fox.

Yy

Y is for yak.

Zz

Z is for zebra.

Games

Hop Along

Make a set of 6" (15 cm) tagboard squares. Write a letter (lower case or capital) on each card. Tape the cards on the floor. They may be placed in alphabetical order or mixed up. Have students hop from card to card, naming each letter and/or giving its sound as they step on it.

Variation: Teacher or another student calls out a letter or sound. Student must hop and stop on the card.

The Initial Game

Ask "What letter does your first name begin with?" "What letter does your last name begin with?" Explain that these letters are called *initials*. Write a letter on the chalkboard and say "Stand up if this letter is the initial of your first name." Repeat until you have covered all the initials in your classroom.

Write your first and last name on the chalkboard and underline the first letter in each word. Remind children that these letters are called *initials*. Call up several children to write their names on the chalkboard (you can do only first names if you wish). Have them underline their initials. Repeat until everyone has a turn.

Make a set of cards with the initials of each child in class. Show one card at a time and have that person come up to get his/her card.

Fun with the Alphabet EMC 774

Bean Bag Toss

Preparations:

Make a game board on a large sheet of posterboard. Use a wide, black felt marker to divide the board into 12 boxes. Write a letter (all capitals or all lower case) in each box. Provide a beanbag. Place the board on the floor. Use masking tape to mark a line a short distance from the board.

Play:

A student stands behind the line and tosses the beanbag at the board. The player gives the name (or sound) of any letter the beanbag is touching. Then the next player gets a turn. If you want to keep score, provide a supply of counters. Players get one counter for each correct answer.

You can make a more challenging game by providing a set of cards containing the same letters as are on the playing board. Students pull a card out of a bag or box and try to toss the beanbag onto that letter. (You might put capital letters on the cards and lower case letters on the card.)

I Spy

This old familiar game can be used to practice recognizing letter names and sounds. Teacher should be "It" to model the game. Say "I spy something that starts with the sound (name a sound). Write the letter making that sound on the chalkboard so students connect the letter with its sound. Students look around the room and try to find what you have "spied." When students show they clearly understand how to play the game, select a child to be "It."

Alphabet Centers

Centers provide an excellent place for independent practice with letters and/or sounds. Before students begin any center activity:

1. Show what the center contains and model how it is to be used.

2. Set center standards:

- What amount of time can be spent at the center?
- How many students may use it at one time?
- What "on-task" behaviors do you expect to see?
- What clean-up procedures must be followed?

Observe students as they work and play at the centers. This will give you a good idea of how much a student knows and any areas needing additional instruction.

Find the Alphabet

Materials:

- a pile of old magazines and catalogs
- large sheets of construction paper
- scissors
- paste
- waste basket (for scraps)

Task:

1. Students look for a specified letter, cutting out all the examples they can find and pasting them on the construction paper.

2. Students look for one example of each letter of the alphabet and paste them on the construction paper.

Letters in the Sand

Materials:

Make a set of letter cards containing the letters you wish students to practice. Supply a flat container of damp sand.

Task:

1. Students look at the card and trace the same letter in the sand several times.
2. Students practice writing their names in the sand.

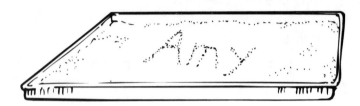

Make a Match - Capital and Lower Case Letters

Materials:

Make two sets of letter cards - one with capital letters and one with lower case letters. (You can use the cards on pages 279 - 304). Laminate the cards.

Task:

Students match the lower case letter with its capital.

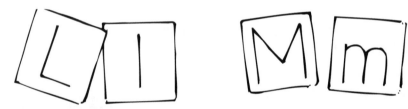

Make a Match - Pictures and Letters

Materials:

Make a set of picture cards and a set of letter cards. (You can use the letters and pictures on pages 279 - 304.) Laminate the cards.

Task:

Students match all the pictures that begin with a specific letter to the letter card.

Alphabet Soup

Materials:

Provide a bowl of Alpha-Bits® cereal letters. Put sheets of construction paper and glue sticks at the center.

Task:

Students can use the letters in a variety of ways:

1. Find all of the letters in their name and glue them to the constrution paper.

2. Use the letters to spell words.

3. Find all of the letters in the alphabet and glue them to the paper.

Make a Word

Materials:

Make a set of picture cards for three-letter, short vowel words (cat, mop, hat, net, etc.). Make the cards self-checking by writing the word on the back of its picture card. Make letter cards providing multiples of commonly used letters. Put the cards in muffin tins to keep the letters separate and easy to find.

Task:

Students look at a picture card, name it, and find the letters as they sound it out. They lay the letters in order under the picture card. They check their answer by turning the picture card over and matching the word with their spelling.

Alphabet Worm

Materials:

Reproduce the patterns on page 278. Use the patterns to cut out a head, tail, and 26 segments out of colored construction paper for your "alphabet worm." Laminate and cut out the pieces. Place the pieces in a sturdy envelope.

Task:

Students put the pieces together in alphabetical order to make the "alphabet worm."

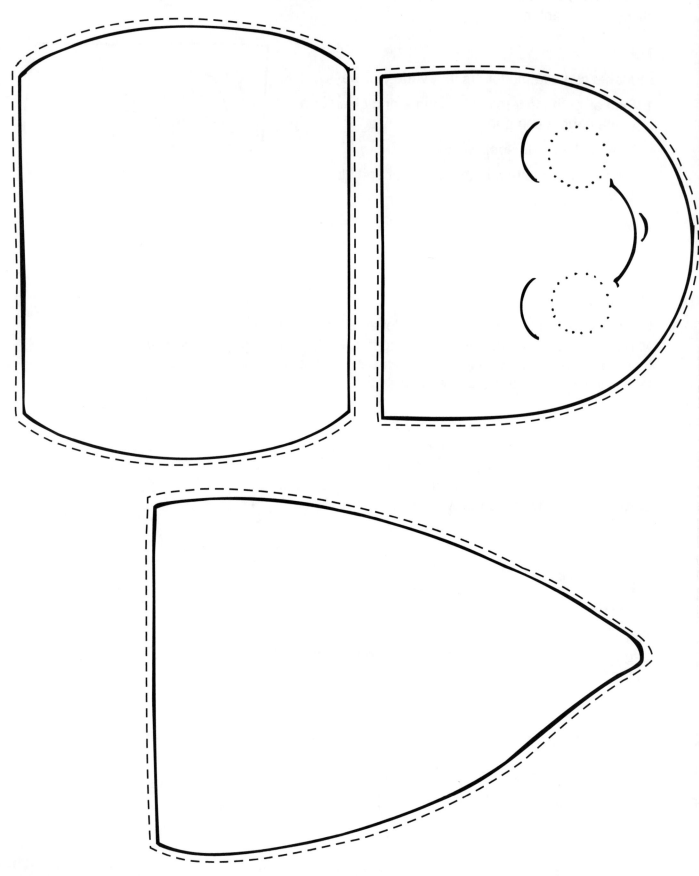

Note: This page contains both long "a" and short "a" words. Use them together or at different times.

A a

Fun with the Alphabet EMC 774

B b

280

C c

D d

E e

Fun with the Alphabet EMC 774

285

Fun with the Alphabet EMC 774

289

Fun with the Alphabet EMC 774

M m

N   n

Fun with the Alphabet EMC 774

Note: This page contains both long "o" and short "o" words. Use them together or at different times.

P p

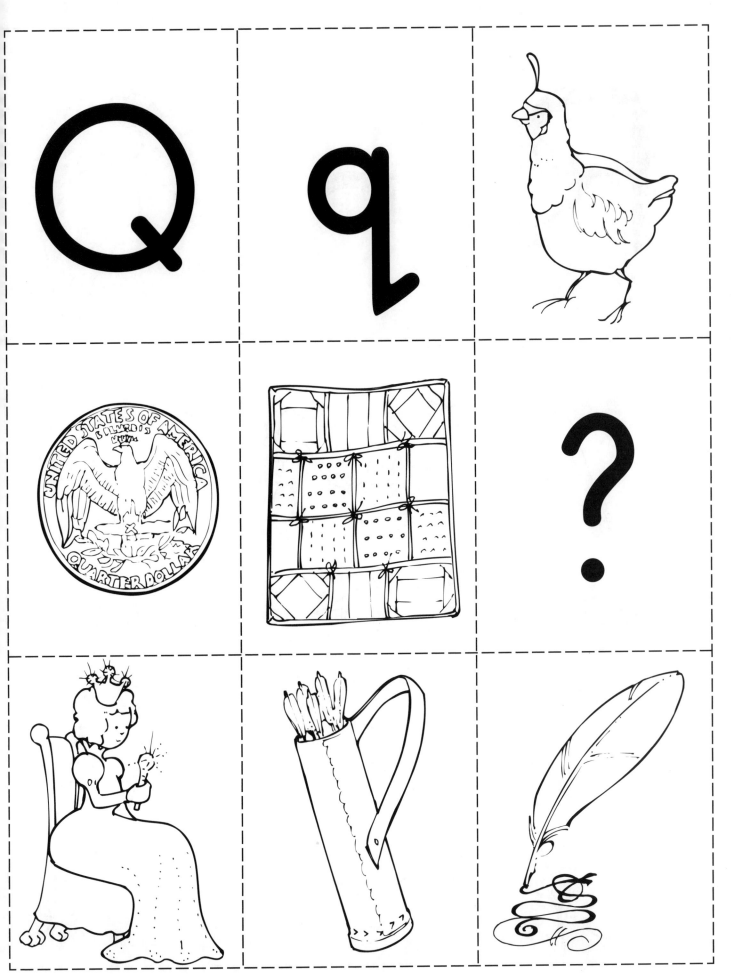

295

R r

S s

Fun with the Alphabet EMC 774

Note: This page contains long "u" and short "u" words. Use them together or at different times.

U u

302

303

Z z